SLOW COOKER DUMP DINNERS & DESSERTS

150 Crazy Yummy Meals for Your Crazy Busy Life

HOPE COMERFORD

Photos by Bonnie Matthews

Good Books

New York, New York

Good Books books may be purchased in bulk at special discounts for sales promotion, corporate gifts, fund-raising, or educational purposes. Special editions can also be created to specifications. For details, contact the Special Sales Department, Good Books, 307 West 36th Street, 11th Floor, New York, NY 10018 or info@skyhorsepublishing.com.

Good Books is an imprint of Skyhorse Publishing, Inc.®, a Delaware corporation.

Visit our website at www.goodbooks.com.

10 9 8 7 6 5 4 3

Library of Congress Cataloging-in-Publication Data is available on file.

Cover design by Mona Lin
Cover photo by Bonnie Matthews

Print ISBN: 978-1-68099-349-3
Ebook ISBN: 978-1-68099-352-3

Printed in China

Table of Contents

Welcome to Fix-It and Forget-It Slow Cooker Dump Dinners & Desserts

You might be thinking, "What on earth is a dump dinner?" and "What on earth is dump dessert?" I'm here to tell you they're the easy recipes you can dump in your slow cooker and go!

Dump dinners require very little prep, no browning, no sautéing, and no searing! You literally just dump the ingredients into your crock and get on with your day. Come dinnertime, you have an amazing dinner waiting for you that took no time at all to get going in the morning.

A dump dessert is basically one that can be made with very little effort, can be made in a single bowl and then dumped into the crock to bake. Sounds easy enough, right? Well, it is just that easy! We'll cook them low and slow, which will make the end result a delicious dessert everyone will adore. (And they won't even know how little effort you put into it!)

Each easy recipe in this book is accompanied by a full-color photo so you know what the end result will hold. You'll find all of these recipes to be full of flavor, but free of hassle! So, take that slow cooker out, find a recipe that looks and sounds wonderful, and get dumping!

A Few Things You Should Know About Your Slow Cooker . . .

Not all slow cookers are created equal . . . or work equally as well for everyone!

Those of us who use slow cookers frequently know we have our own preferences when it comes to which slow cooker we choose to use. For instance, I love my programmable slow cooker, but there are many programmable slow cookers I've tried that I've strongly disliked. Why? Because some go by increments of 15 or 30 minutes and some go by 4, 6, 8, or 10 hours. I dislike those restrictions, but I have family and friends who don't mind them at all! I am also pretty brand loyal when it comes to my manual slow cookers because I've had great success with those and have had unsuccessful moments with slow cookers of other brands. So, which slow cooker(s) is/are best for your household?

It really depends on how many people you're feeding and if you're gone for long periods of time. Here are my recommendations:

For 2–3 person household	3–5 quart slow cooker
For 4–5 person household	5–6 quart slow cooker
For a 6+ person household	6½–7 quart slow cooker

Large slow cooker advantages/disadvantages:

- Advantages:
  - You can fit a loaf pan or a baking dish into a 6- or 7-quart, depending on the shape of your cooker. That allows you to make bread or cakes, or even smaller quantities of main dishes. (Take your favorite baking dish and loaf pan along when you shop for a cooker to make sure they'll fit inside.)
  - You can feed large groups of people, or make larger quantities of food, allowing for leftovers, or meals, to freeze.
- Disadvantages:
  - They take up more storage room.
  - They don't fit as neatly into a dishwasher.
  - If your crock isn't ⅔–¾ full, you may burn your food.

Small slow cooker advantages/disadvantages:

- Advantages:
  - They're great for lots of appetizers, for serving hot drinks, for baking cakes straight in the crock, and for dorm rooms or apartments.
  - Great option for making recipes of smaller quantities.
- Disadvantages:
  - Food in smaller quantities tends to cook more quickly than larger amounts. So keep an eye on it.
  - Chances are, you won't have many leftovers. So, if you like to have leftovers, a smaller slow cooker may not be a good option for you.

My recommendation:

Have at least two slow cookers; one around 3 to 4 quarts and one 6 quarts or larger. A third would be a huge bonus (and a great advantage to your cooking repertoire!). The advantage of having at least a couple is you can make a larger variety of recipes. Also, you can make at least two or three dishes at once for a whole meal.

Manual vs. Programmable

If you are gone for only six to eight hours a day, a manual slow cooker might be just fine for you. If you are gone for more than eight hours during the day, I would highly recommend purchasing a programmable slow cooker that will switch to warm when the cook time you set is up. It will allow you to cook a wider variety of recipes.

The two I use most frequently are my 4-quart manual slow cooker and my 6½-quart programmable slow cooker. I like that I can make smaller portions in my 4-quart slow cooker on days I don't need or want leftovers, but I also love how my 6½-quart slow cooker can accommodate whole chickens, turkey breasts, hams, or big batches of soups. I use them both often.

Get to Know Your Slow Cooker . . .

Plan a little time to get acquainted with your slow cooker. Each slow cooker has its own personality—just like your oven (and your car). Plus, many new slow cookers cook hotter and faster than earlier models. I think that with all of the concern for food safety, the slow cooker manufacturers have amped up their settings so that "High," "Low," and "Warm" are all higher temperatures than in the older models. That means they cook hotter—and therefore, faster—than the first slow cookers. The beauty of these little machines is that they're supposed to cook low and slow. We count on that when we flip the switch in the morning before we leave the house for ten hours or so. So, because none of us knows what kind of temperament our slow cooker has until we try it out, nor how hot it cooks—don't assume anything. Save yourself a disappointment and make the first recipe in your new slow cooker on a day when you're at home. Cook it for the shortest amount of time the recipe calls for. Then, check the food to see if it's done. Or if you start smelling food that seems to be finished, turn off the cooker and rescue your food.

Also, all slow cookers seem to have a "hot spot," which is of great importance to know, especially when baking with your slow cooker. This spot may tend to burn food in that area if you're not careful. If you're baking directly in your slow cooker, I recommend covering the "hot spot" with some foil.

Tips and Tricks

Slow cookers tend to work best when they're ⅔ to ¾ of the way full. You may need to increase the cooking time if you've exceeded that amount, or reduce it if you've put in less than that. If you're going to exceed that limit, it would be best to reduce the recipe, or split it between two slow cookers. (Remember how I suggested owning at least two or three slow cookers?)

Keep your veggies on the bottom. That puts them in more direct contact with the heat. The fuller your slow cooker, the longer it will take its contents to cook. Also, the more densely packed the cooker's contents are, the longer they will take to cook. And finally, the larger the chunks of meat or vegetables, the more time they will need to cook.

Keep the lid on! Every time you take a peek, you lose 20 minutes of cooking time. Please take this into consideration each time you lift the lid! I know, some of you can't help yourself and are going to lift anyway. Just don't forget to tack on 20 minutes to your cook time for each time you peeked!

Sometimes it's beneficial to remove the lid. If you'd like your dish to thicken a bit, take the lid off during the last half hour to hour of cooking time.

If you have a big slow cooker (7- to 8-quart), you can cook a small batch in it by putting the recipe ingredients into an oven-safe baking dish or baking pan and then placing that into the cooker's crock. First, put a trivet or some metal jar rings on the bottom of the crock, and then set your dish or pan on top of them. Or a loaf pan may "hook onto" the top ridges of the crock belonging to a large oval cooker and hang there straight and securely, "baking" a cake or quick bread. Cover the cooker and flip it on.

The outside of your slow cooker will be hot! Please remember to keep it out of reach of children and keep that in mind for yourself as well!

Get yourself a quick-read meat thermometer and use it! This helps remove the question of whether or not your meat is fully cooked, and helps prevent you from overcooking your meat as well.

- Internal Cooking Temperatures:
    - Beef—125–130°F (rare); 140–145°F (medium); 160°F (well-done)
    - Pork—140–145°F (rare); 145–150°F (medium); 160°F (well-done)
    - Turkey and Chicken—165°F

Frozen meat: The basic rule of thumb is, don't put frozen meat into the slow cooker. The meat does not reach the proper internal temperature in time. This especially applies to thick cuts of meat! Proceed with caution!

Add fresh herbs 10 minutes before the end of the cooking time to maximize their flavor.

If your recipe calls for cooked pasta, add it 10 minutes before the end of the cooking time if the cooker is on High; 30 minutes before the end of the cooking time if it's on Low. Then the pasta won't get mushy.

If your recipe calls for sour cream or cream, stir it in 5 minutes before the end of the cooking time. You want it to heat but not boil or simmer.

- Approximate Slow Cooker Temperatures (Remember, each slow cooker is different):
    - High—212°F–300°F
    - Low—170°F–200°F
    - Simmer—185°F
    - Warm—165°F

- Cooked beans freeze well. Store them in freezer bags (squeeze the air out first) or freezer boxes. Cooked and dried bean measurements:
    - 16-oz. can, drained = about 1¾ cups beans
    - 19-oz. can, drained = about 2 cups beans
    - 1 lb. dried beans (about 2½ cups) = 5 cups cooked beans

Dump Soups, Stews, Chilies & Chowders

Black Bean Soup with Chicken and Salsa

Makes 4–6 servings

Hope Comerford, Clinton Township, MI

Prep. Time: 10 minutes ⚇ *Cooking Time: 6–8 hours* ⚇ *Ideal Slow Cooker Size: 5- to 6-qt.*

4 cups chicken broth

1 large boneless, skinless chicken breast

2 15-oz. cans black beans, drained and rinsed

16-oz. jar salsa

1 cup frozen corn

1 cup sliced fresh mushrooms

½ red onion, chopped

1 jalapeño pepper (whole)

1½ tsp. cumin

salt to taste

pepper to taste

Optional Toppings:

shredded cheese, sour cream, cilantro, avocado.

1. Place all ingredients except the toppings in slow cooker. Stir.

2. Cover and cook on Low for 6–8 hours.

3. Remove the chicken and shred between two forks. Replace back in the soup and stir.

Variation:

You may chop up the jalapeño for extra heat. Leaving it whole provides the flavor without the heat.

Serving suggestion:

Serve garnished with the optional toppings.

Chicken and Corn Soup

Makes 4–6 servings

Eleanor Larson, Glen Lyon, PA

Prep. Time: 15 minutes ⚜ *Cooking Time: 8–9 hours* ⚜ *Ideal slow-cooker size: 4-qt.*

2 whole boneless, skinless chicken breasts, cubed
1 onion, chopped
1 garlic clove, minced
2 carrots, sliced
2 ribs celery, chopped
2 medium potatoes, cubed
1 tsp. mixed dried herbs
⅓ cup tomato sauce
12-oz. can cream-style corn
14-oz. can whole kernel corn
3 cups chicken stock
¼ cup chopped Italian parsley
1 tsp. salt
¼ tsp. pepper

1. Combine all ingredients except parsley, salt, and pepper in slow cooker.

2. Cover. Cook on Low 8–9 hours, or until chicken is tender.

3. Add parsley and seasonings 30 minutes before serving

Easy Chicken Tortilla Soup

Makes 6–8 servings

Becky Harder, Monument, CO

Prep. Time: 5–10 minutes ⚓ *Cooking Time: 8 hours* ⚓ *Ideal slow-cooker size: 4- to 5-qt.*

4 chicken breast halves

2 15-oz. cans black beans, undrained

2 15-oz. cans Mexican stewed tomatoes, or Ro*Tel tomatoes

1 cup salsa (mild, medium, or hot, whichever you prefer)

4-oz. can chopped green chilies

14½-oz. can tomato sauce

tortilla chips

1. Combine all ingredients in large slow cooker.

2. Cover. Cook on Low 8 hours.

3. Just before serving, remove chicken breasts and slice into bite-sized pieces. Stir into soup.

4. Put a handful of tortilla chips in each individual soup bowl. Ladle soup over chips. Top with shredded cheese.

White Chicken Chili

Makes 8 servings

Lucille Hollinger, Richland, PA

Prep. Time: 10 minutes ♣ *Cooking Time: 5–6 hours* ♣ *Ideal slow-cooker size: 3-qt.*

4 cups cubed cooked chicken
2 cups chicken broth
2 14½-oz. cans cannellini beans
14½-oz. can garbanzo beans
1 cup shredded white cheddar cheese
¼ cup chopped onion
¼ cup chopped bell pepper
2 tsp. ground cumin
½ tsp. dried oregano
¼ tsp. cayenne pepper
¼ tsp. salt

1. Combine all ingredients in slow cooker.

2. Cover and cook on Low for 5–6 hours.

Variations:

Omit garbanzo beans. Shred chicken instead of cubing it. Add 1 tsp. Italian herb seasoning.
—Beverly Hummel

Good go-alongs with this recipe: Cornbread and salad.

TIP
Serve with sour cream, shredded cheese, and tortilla chips.

Chicken Barley Chili

Makes 10 servings

Colleen Heatwole, Burton, MI

Prep. Time: 20 minutes ⚭ *Cooking Time: 6–8 hours* ⚭ *Ideal slow-cooker size: 6-qt.*

2 14½-oz. cans diced tomatoes

16-oz. jar salsa

1 cup quick-cooking barley, uncooked

3 cups water

1¾ cups chicken stock

15½-oz. can black beans, rinsed and drained

3 cups cubed cooked chicken or turkey

15¼-oz. can whole-kernel corn, undrained

1–3 tsp. chili powder, depending on how hot you like your chili

1 tsp. cumin

1 tsp. salt

⅛ tsp. pepper

1. Combine all ingredients in slow cooker.

2. Cover. Cook on Low 6–8 hours, or until barley is tender.

Serving suggestion:
Serve in individual soup bowls topped with sour cream and shredded cheese.

Very Shroomy Chicken Stew

Makes: 4–6 servings

Carolyn Spohn, Shawnee, KS

Prep. Time: 15 minutes ☙ Cooking Time: 4–6 hours ☙ Ideal slow-cooker size: 5-qt.

1 large boneless chicken breast in 1-inch cubes

10¾-oz. can cream of chicken soup

10¾-oz. can cream of mushroom soup

1 cup sliced mushrooms

1 cup frozen mixed vegetables

2 Tbsp. dried minced onion

2 tsp. fresh minced garlic

1 or 2 tsp. dried rosemary leaves

1 tsp. dried oregano leaves

1. Place all ingredients in slow cooker; stir to mix.

2. Cover and cook on Low 4–6 hours.

Serving suggestion:
Serve over noodles or rice.

Creamy Potato Chowder

Makes 8 servings

Emily Fox, Bernville, PA

Prep. Time: 15 minutes ⚜ *Cooking Time: 8 hours* ⚜ *Ideal slow-cooker size: 5-qt.*

8 cups diced potaoes

5½ cups chicken broth

10½ oz. can cream of chicken soup

⅓ cup chopped onion

¼ tsp. pepper

8 oz. cream cheese, cubed

½ lb. bacon, cooked and crumbled

minced chives

1. Combine the first five ingredients in the crock.

2. Cover and cook on Low 8–10 hours.

3. Add cream cheese; stir until blended. Garnish with bacon and chives.

Steak and Wild Rice Soup

Makes 6 servings

Sally Holzem, Schofield, WI

Prep. Time: 15 minutes ⚘ *Cooking Time: 5 hours* ⚘ *Ideal slow-cooker size: 5-qt.*

4 cups beef stock

3 cups cubed cooked roast beef

4 oz. sliced fresh mushrooms

½ cup chopped onion

¼ cup ketchup

2 tsp. cider vinegar

1 tsp. brown sugar

1 tsp. Worcestershire sauce

⅛ tsp. ground mustard

1½ cups cooked wild rice

1 cup frozen peas

1. Combine stock, beef, mushrooms, onion, ketchup, vinegar, sugar, Worcestershire sauce, and mustard in slow cooker.

2. Cook on Low 4 hours.

3. Add rice and peas. Cook an additional hour on Low.

Good go-alongs with this recipe:
    Crusty rolls and a green salad.

TIP

Great way to use up scraps of meat and broth left from a roast beef, and a nice way to transform leftover wild rice.

Beef Vegetable Soup

Makes 6 servings

Anona M. Teel, Bangor, PA

Prep. Time: 15 minutes ❧ *Cooking Time: 8–10 hours* ❧ *Ideal slow-cooker size: 6½-qt.*

1–1½-lb. soup bone
1 lb. stewing beef cubes
1½ qts. cold water
1 Tbsp. salt
¾ cup diced celery
¾ cup diced carrots
¾ cup diced potatoes
¾ cup diced onion
1 cup frozen mixed vegetables of your choice
16-oz. can diced tomatoes
⅛ tsp. pepper
1 Tbsp. chopped dried parsley

1. Put all ingredients in slow cooker.

2. Cover. Cook on Low 8–10 hours. Remove bone before serving.

Minestrone Soup

Makes 8 servings

Dorothy Shank, Sterling, IL

Prep. Time: 10 minutes ⚓ *Cooking Time: 4–12 hours* ⚓ *Ideal slow-cooker size: 4- to 5-qt.*

3 cups beef stock

1 ½ lbs. stewing meat, cut into bite-sized pieces

1 medium onion, diced

4 carrots, diced

14½-oz. can diced tomatoes

1 tsp. salt

10-oz. pkg. frozen mixed vegetables, or your choice of frozen vegetables

1 Tbsp. dried basil

½ cup dry vermicelli

1 tsp. dried oregano

1. Combine all ingredients in slow cooker. Stir well.

2. Cover. Cook on Low 10–12 hours, or on High 4–5 hours.

Serving suggestion:
Top individual servings with grated Parmesan cheese.

Chipotle Beef Chili

Makes 8 servings

Karen Ceneviva, Seymour, CT

Prep. Time: 10–15 minutes ⚬ Cooking Time: 4–9 hours ⚬ Ideal slow-cooker size: 3½-qt.

16-oz. jar chunky chipotle salsa
1 cup water
2 tsp. chili powder
1 tsp. salt
1 large onion, chopped
2 lbs. stewing beef, cut into ½-inch pieces
19-oz. can red kidney beans, drained and rinsed

1. Stir all ingredients together in slow cooker.

2. Cover. Cook on High 4–5 hours or on Low 8–9 hours, until beef is fork-tender.

Beef Stew

Makes 10 servings

Carol Eveleth, Hillsdale, WY

Prep. Time: 20 minutes ⚬ Cooking Time: 5–7 hours ⚬ Ideal slow-cooker size: 5-qt.

2-lb. boneless beef chuck roast, cut into 1-inch chunks

6 large carrots, sliced, chopped

4 medium potatoes, peeled or not, chopped

4 ribs celery, sliced, chopped

1 large onion, chopped

3 tsp. salt

¼ tsp. black pepper

3 Tbsp. quick-cooking tapioca

½ cup ketchup

1 cup tomato juice

1 cup water

1. Grease interior of slow cooker crock.

2. Place beef, carrots, potatoes, celery, and onion in crock.

3. Sprinkle seasonings and tapioca on top.

4. Pour ketchup, tomato juice, and water over all. Stir everything together well.

5. Cover. Cook for 5–7 hours on Low, or until instant-read meat thermometer registers 145°F when stuck in center of beef chunks and vegetables are as tender as you like them.

Tuscan Beef Stew

Makes 12 servings

Orpha Herr, Andover, NY

Prep. Time: 20 minutes ❧ *Cooking Time: 8–9 hours* ❧ *Ideal slow-cooker size: 6-qt.*

10¾-oz. can tomato soup

1½ cups beef broth

½ cup burgundy wine or other red wine

1 tsp. Italian herb seasoning

½ tsp. garlic powder

14½-oz. can diced Italian-style tomatoes, undrained

½ cup diced onion

3 large carrots, cut in 1-inch pieces

2 lbs. stew beef, cut into 1-inch pieces

2 16-oz. cans cannellini beans, rinsed and drained

1. Stir soup, broth, wine, Italian seasoning, garlic powder, tomatoes, onion, carrots, and beef into slow cooker.

2. Cover and cook on Low 8–9 hours or until vegetables are tender-crisp.

3. Stir in beans. Turn to High until heated through, 10–20 minutes more.

Hearty Potato Sauerkraut Soup

Makes 6–8 servings

Kathy Hertzler, Lancaster, PA

Prep. Time: 15–20 minutes ⚜ *Cooking Time: 10–12 hours* ⚜ *Ideal slow-cooker size: 4-qt.*

4 cups chicken broth

10¾-oz. can cream of mushroom soup

16-oz. can sauerkraut, rinsed and drained

8 oz. fresh mushrooms, sliced

1 medium potato, cubed

2 medium carrots, peeled and sliced

2 ribs celery, chopped

2 lbs. Polish kielbasa (smoked), cubed

2½ cups chopped, cooked chicken

2 Tbsp. vinegar

2 tsp. dried dillweed

1½ tsp. pepper

1. Combine all ingredients in large slow cooker.

2. Cover. Cook on Low 10–12 hours.

3. If necessary, skim fat before serving.

Kielbasa Soup

Makes 8 servings

Hope Comerford, Clinton Township, MI

Prep. Time: 10 minutes & Cooking Time: 10 hours & Ideal slow-cooker size: 8-qt.

6-oz. can tomato paste

1 medium onion, chopped

3 medium potatoes, diced

2 cups chopped cabbage

½ cup chopped carrot

½ cup chopped celery

½ cup frozen green chopped green beans

2 lbs. kielbasa, cut into ¼-inch pieces

2 tsp. salt

1 tsp. oregano

1 tsp. thyme

½ tsp. pepper

6 cups water

6 cups chicken stock

1. Combine all ingredients in crock.

2. Cover. Cook on Low 10 hours.

Split Pea Soup

Makes 8 servings

Kelly Amos, Pittsboro, NC

Prep. Time: 10 minutes   ❧   Cooking Time: 8–9 hours   ❧   Ideal slow-cooker size: 4½-qt.

2 cups dry split peas
8 cups water
2 onions, chopped
2 carrots, peeled and sliced
4 slices Canadian bacon, chopped
2 Tbsp. chicken bouillon granules, or 2 chicken bouillon cubes
1 tsp. salt
¼–½ tsp. pepper

1. Combine all ingredients in slow cooker.

2. Cover. Cook on Low 8–9 hours.

Variation:

For a creamier soup, remove half of soup when done and puree. Stir back into rest of soup.

Italian Shredded Pork Stew

Makes: 6–8 servings

Emily Fox, Bernville, PA

Prep. Time: 20 minutes ❧ Cooking Time: 8 hours ❧ Ideal slow-cooker size: 5-qt.

2 medium sweet potatoes, peeled and cubed

2 cups chopped fresh kale

1 large onion, chopped

3 cloves garlic, minced

2½–3½ lb. boneless pork shoulder butt roast

14-oz. can white kidney or cannellini beans, drained

1½ tsp. Italian seasoning

½ tsp. salt

½ tsp. pepper

3 14½-oz. cans chicken broth

sour cream, *optional*

1. Place first four ingredients in slow cooker.

2. Place roast on vegetables.

3. Add beans and seasonings.

4. Pour the broth over top.

5. Cover and cook on Low 8–10 hours or until meat is tender.

6. Remove meat. Skim fat from cooking juices if desired. Shred pork with two forks and return to cooker. Heat through.

7. Garnish with sour cream if desired.

Ham and Bean Stew

Makes 4–6 servings

Sharon Wantland, Menomonee Falls, WI

Prep. Time: 15 minutes & Cooking Time: 5–7 hours & Ideal slow-cooker size: 3-qt.

2 16-oz. cans baked beans
2 medium potatoes, peeled and cubed
2 cups cubed ham
2 ribs celery, chopped
1 onion, chopped
½ cup water
1 Tbsp. cider vinegar
1 tsp. salt
⅛ tsp. pepper

1. In a slow cooker combine all ingredients. Mix well.

2. Cover and cook on Low for 5–7 hours, or until the potatoes are tender.

Manhattan Clam Chowder

Makes 8 servings

Joyce Slaymaker, Strasburg, PA
Louise Stackhouse, Benton, PA

Prep. Time: 15 minutes ☙ *Cooking Time: 8–10 hours* ☙ *Ideal slow-cooker size: 3½-qt.*

¼ lb. salt pork, or bacon, diced and fried
1 large onion, chopped
2 carrots, thinly sliced
3 ribs celery, sliced
1 Tbsp. dried parsley flakes
28-oz. can tomatoes
½ tsp. salt
2–3 8-oz. cans clams with liquid
2 whole peppercorns
1 bay leaf
1½ tsp. dried crushed thyme
3 medium potatoes, cubed

1. Combine all ingredients in slow cooker.

2. Cover. Cook on Low 8–10 hours. Remove bay leaf before serving.

All-Vegetable Soup

Makes 8–10 servings

Jean Harris Robinson, Pemberton, NJ

Prep. Time: 25 minutes ❧ Cooking Time: 4–6 hours ❧ Ideal slow-cooker size: 4-qt.

2 Tbsp. olive oil

1 large white onion, Vidalia preferred, diced

2 medium carrots, diced

2 cloves garlic, minced

20-oz. pkg. frozen cubed butternut squash, or 4 cups chopped fresh

2 cups finely chopped cabbage

1 cup chopped kale, packed

½ tsp. ground allspice

¼ tsp. ground ginger, or 1 Tbsp. finely grated fresh ginger

4 sprigs fresh thyme, or 1 tsp. dried thyme

1 tsp. salt, or to taste

14-oz. can diced tomatoes with juice

1 qt. no-salt vegetable broth

1. Combine all ingredients in cooker.

2. Cook on Low 4–6 hours until veggies are soft.

Good go-alongs with this recipe:
Add a dollop of Greek yogurt to the top of each bowl. Place some hot cooked grains, such as brown rice or quinoa, in soup bowls before ladling in soup.

TIP

Refrigerate for several days or freeze for later. It is a family pleaser. I like to prep the vegetables the night before. I often use frozen vegetables and sometimes add leftover green beans or broccoli at the last minute before serving.

Fresh Tomato Soup

Makes 6 servings

Rebecca Leichty, Harrisonburg, VA

Prep. Time: 20–25 minutes ♧ *Cooking Time: 3–4 hours* ♧ *Ideal slow-cooker size: 3½- or 4-qt.*

5 cups ripe tomatoes, diced (your choice about whether or not to peel them)

1 Tbsp. tomato paste

4 cups salt-free chicken broth

1 carrot, grated

1 onion, minced

1 Tbsp. garlic, minced

1 tsp. dried basil

pepper to taste

2 Tbsp. lemon juice

1 bay leaf

1. Combine all ingredients in a slow cooker.

2. Cook on Low for 3–4 hours. Stir once while cooking.

3. Remove bay leaf before serving.

Red Lentil Soup

Makes 4–6 servings

Carolyn Spohn, Shawnee, KS

Prep. Time: 20 minutes ⚘ *Cooking Time: 3–4 hours* ⚘ *Ideal slow-cooker size: 5-qt.*

¾ cup red lentils

½ cup brown rice, uncooked

4 cups vegetable broth

1 small potato, diced

2 medium carrots, chopped

1 small onion, chopped

2 cloves garlic, chopped

½ tsp. turmeric

¼ tsp. ground cumin

¼ tsp. ground coriander

salt and pepper, to taste

plain yogurt, for serving

1. Combine all ingredients except plain yogurt in slow cooker.

2. Cover and cook on High for 3–4 hours, until vegetables are soft.

3. Puree with immersion blender until smooth.

4. Serve in bowls with a little plain yogurt dolloped on top.

Variations:

Sprinkle with chopped cilantro.

Good go-alongs with this recipe:

Pita bread and a green salad.

TIP

Other orange-colored vegetables can be used with or instead of carrots. Red or orange sweet peppers and/or butternut squash are good. This is a very flexible soup, as you can vary the vegetables according to what you have on hand.

Cream of Broccoli and Mushroom Soup

Makes 12 servings

Leona Miller, Millersburg, OH

Prep. Time: 20 minutes ⚶ Cooking Time: 3½–8 hours ⚶ Ideal slow-cooker size: 5- or 6-qt.

8 oz. fresh mushrooms, sliced

2 lbs. fresh broccoli, chopped

3 10¾-oz. cans cream of broccoli soup

½ tsp. dried thyme leaves, crushed, *optional*

3 bay leaves, *optional*

1 pint half-and-half

4 oz. extra-lean smoked ham, chopped

¼ tsp. black pepper

1. Combine all ingredients in slow cooker.

2. Cook on Low 4–5 hours or on High 2–3 hours.

3. Remove bay leaves before serving, if using.

Creamy Pumpkin Soup

Makes 6 servings

Janeen Troyer, Fairview, MI

Prep. Time: 10 minutes ∿ Cooking Time: 2½ hours ∿ Ideal slow-cooker size: 4-qt.

29-oz. can pumpkin
2 15-oz. cans chicken broth
⅛ tsp. ground nutmeg
¼ tsp. ground allspice
½ tsp. curry powder
⅛ tsp. ground ginger
1 cup cream, at room temperature

1. In slow cooker, mix pumpkin, broth, and spices.

2. Cover and cook on High for 1½ hours and then turn to Low for 1 hour.

3. Add cream 20 minutes before serving.

Sweet Potato Lentil Soup

Makes 6 servings

Joleen Albrecht, Gladstone, MI

Prep. Time: 10–15 minutes ⚘ *Cooking Time: 6 hours* ⚘ *Ideal slow-cooker size: 4-qt.*

4 cups vegetable broth

3 cups (about 1¼ lbs.) sweet potatoes, peeled and cubed

3 medium carrots, chopped

1 medium onion, chopped

4 cloves garlic, minced

1 cup dried lentils, rinsed

½ tsp. ground cumin

¼ tsp. salt

¼ tsp. cayenne pepper

¼ tsp. ground ginger

¼ cup fresh cilantro, minced, or 1–2 Tbsp. dried cilantro

1. Combine all ingredients in slow cooker.

2. Cover. Cook on Low 6 hours, or until vegetables are done to your liking.

6-Can Soup

Makes 8 servings

Audrey L. Kneer, Williamsfield, IL

Prep. Time: 10 minutes   &   Cooking Time: 3–4 hours   &   Ideal slow-cooker size: 3½- or 4-qt.

10¾-oz. can tomato soup
15-oz. can whole-kernel corn, drained
15-oz. can mixed vegetables, drained
15-oz. can chili beans, undrained
14½-oz. can diced tomatoes, undrained
14½-oz. can chicken broth

1. Combine all ingredients in slow cooker.
2. Cover. Cook on Low 3–4 hours.

Black Bean Chili

Makes 8 servings

Joyce Cox, Port Angeles, WA

Prep. Time: 20 minutes ⚬ *Cooking Time: 6–8 hours* ⚬ *Ideal slow-cooker size: 6-qt.*

1½ cups fresh-brewed coffee
1½ cups vegetable broth
2 15-oz. cans diced tomatoes with juice
15-oz. can tomato sauce
8 cups cooked black beans, drained
1 medium yellow onion, diced
4 cloves garlic, minced
2 Tbsp. brown sugar, packed
2 Tbsp. chili powder
1 Tbsp. ground cumin
salt to taste

1. Combine all ingredients except salt in slow cooker.

2. Cover and cook on Low for 6–8 hours. Add salt near end of cooking.

Variations:

Use 4 15-oz. cans of black beans, rinsed and drained, instead of the 8 cups cooked black beans. Mash some of the beans with a potato masher before adding to cooker. The chili will be thicker.

TIP
Great served in bowls with cilantro, cubed avocados, Greek yogurt or sour cream, and grated cheese on top.

Potato and Corn Chowder

Makes 6 servings

Genelle Taylor, Perrysburg, OH

Prep. Time: 20 minutes ⚜ Cooking Time: 3–8 hours ⚜ Ideal slow-cooker size: 6-qt.

3 cups red potatoes, diced

16-oz. pkg. frozen corn

3 Tbsp. flour

6 cups chicken stock

1 tsp. dried thyme

1 tsp. dried oregano

½ tsp. garlic powder

½ tsp. onion powder

Kosher salt and freshly ground black pepper, to taste

2 Tbsp. butter

¼ cup heavy cream

1. Place potatoes and corn in slow cooker. Stir in flour and toss gently to combine.

2. Stir in chicken stock, thyme, oregano, garlic powder, onion powder, salt and pepper to taste.

3. Cover and cook on Low for 7–8 hours or High for 3–4 hours.

4. Stir in butter and heavy cream.

5. Serve immediately.

TIP
Cooking time may need to be adjusted depending on size of diced potatoes.

Chicken and Turkey
Dump Dinners

Salsa Ranch Chicken with Black Beans

Makes 8 servings

Hope Comerford, Clinton Township, MI

Prep. Time: 10 minutes ❧ Cooking Time: 5–6 hours ❧ Ideal slow-cooker size: 3-qt.

2 large boneless, skinless chicken breasts

1 oz. packet low-sodium taco seasoning

1 oz. packet dry ranch dressing mix

1 cup salsa

10½-oz. can condensed cream of chicken soup

15-oz. can black beans, drained, rinsed

sour cream, *optional*

shredded cheese, *optional*

1. Place chicken in crock.

2. In a bowl, mix together the taco seasoning, ranch dressing mix, salsa, cream of chicken soup, and black beans. Pour over the chicken.

3. Cover and cook on Low for 5–6 hours.

4. Serve with sour cream and cheese, if desired.

Serving suggestion:
Serve on top of rice or in a tortilla.

Creamy Chicken Rice Casserole

Makes 8 servings

Wanda Roth, Napoleon, OH

Prep. Time: 20 minutes ⚶ *Cooking Time: 2–6 hours* ⚶ *Ideal slow-cooker size: 6-qt.*

I cup long-grain rice, uncooked

3 cups water

2 tsp. low-sodium chicken bouillon granules

10¾-oz. can cream of chicken soup

2 cups chopped, cooked chicken breast

¼ tsp. garlic powder

I tsp. onion salt

I cup grated cheddar cheese

16-oz. bag frozen broccoli, thawed

1. Combine all ingredients except broccoli in slow cooker.

2. Cook on High a total of 2–3 hours or on Low a total of 4–6 hours.

3. One hour before end of cooking time, stir in broccoli.

Chicken and Dumplings

Makes 5–6 servings

Annabelle Unternahrer, Shipshewana, IN

Prep. Time: 25 minutes ⚭ Cooking Time: 2½–3½ hours ⚭ Ideal slow-cooker size: 3- or 4-qt.

1 lb. uncooked boneless, skinless chicken breasts, cut in 1-inch cubes

1 lb. frozen vegetables of your choice

1 medium-sized onion, diced

3 cups chicken broth, divided

1½ cups low-fat buttermilk biscuit mix

1. Combine chicken, vegetables, onion, and chicken broth (reserve ½ cup, plus 1 Tbsp., broth) in slow cooker.

2. Cover. Cook on High 2–3 hours.

3. Mix biscuit mix with reserved broth until moistened. Drop by tablespoonfuls over hot chicken and vegetables.

4. Cover. Cook on High 10 minutes.

5. Uncover. Cook on High 20 minutes more.

6-Can Meal

Makes 4 servings

Shelia Heil, Lancaster, PA

Prep. Time: 5 minutes & *Cooking Time: 1–4 hours* & *Ideal slow-cooker size: 4-qt.*

10½-oz. can cream of chicken soup (undiluted)

10½-oz. can chicken rice soup (undiluted)

14½-oz. can French-cut green beans, drained

7-oz. can cooked chicken

5-oz. can chow mein noodles

6-oz. can french fried onions

1. Mix together all ingredients, then dump in slow cooker.

2. Cover and cook for 4 hours on Low or 1–2 hours on High, so everything is heated through.

Nova Scotia Chicken

Makes 5 servings

Joanne Kennedy, Plattsburgh, NY

Prep. Time: 25 minutes   ♣   *Cooking Time: 5–6 hours*   ♣   *Ideal slow-cooker size: 4-qt.*

4 uncooked boneless, skinless chicken breast halves, cubed

1 medium-sized onion, chopped

1 small-medium-sized green bell pepper, chopped

1 cup chopped celery

1 qt. stewed, or crushed, tomatoes

1 cup water

½ cup tomato paste

2 Tbsp. Worcestershire sauce

2 Tbsp. brown sugar

2 tsp. salt

1 tsp. black pepper

1. Combine all ingredients in slow cooker.

2. Cover. Cook on Low 5–6 hours.

Serving suggestion:
Serve over rice.

Chicken Cacciatore

Makes 10 servings

Dawn Day, Westminster, CA

Prep. Time: 20 minutes ❧ Cooking Time: 5–6 hours ❧ Ideal slow-cooker size: 3-qt.

2 lbs. uncooked boneless, skinless chicken breasts, cubed
½ lb. fresh mushrooms
1 bell pepper, chopped
1 medium-sized onion, chopped
12-oz. can chopped tomatoes
6-oz. can tomato paste
12-oz. can tomato sauce
½ tsp. dried oregano
½ tsp. dried basil
½ tsp. garlic powder
½ tsp. salt
½ tsp. black pepper

1. Combine all ingredients in slow cooker.

2. Cover. Cook on Low 5–6 hours.

Serving suggestion:

Serve over rice or whole wheat, or semolina, pasta.

Chicken Marsala

Makes 4 servings

Genelle Taylor, Perrysburg, OH

Prep. Time: 10 minutes & Cooking Time: 5–6 hours & Ideal slow-cooker size: 5- or 6-qt.

4 boneless, skinless chicken breasts
salt and pepper to taste
2 tsp. minced garlic
1 cup sliced mushrooms
1 cup sweet marsala cooking wine
½ cup water
¼ cup cornstarch
fresh parsley, roughly chopped

1. Lightly grease slow cooker with nonstick spray.

2. Season chicken with salt and pepper and place in slow cooker.

3. Top chicken with garlic, mushrooms, and wine.

4. Cover and cook on Low for 5–6 hours.

5. Transfer chicken to a plate.

6. Whisk together and cornstarch; then stir into slow cooker.

7. Add chicken back into slow cooker, switch heat to High, cover and cook another 20–30 minutes, until sauce is thickened.

8. Add salt and pepper as needed. Sprinkle with parsley and serve.

Chicken Italiano

Makes 6 servings

Mary C. Casey, Scranton, PA

Prep. Time: 15–20 minutes ♣ Cooking Time: 3½–6 hours ♣ Ideal slow-cooker size: 4-qt.

2 large whole boneless, skinless chicken breasts, each cut in 3 pieces

¾ tsp. salt

¼ tsp. black pepper

½ tsp. dried oregano

½ tsp. dried basil

2 bay leaves

26-oz. jar marinara sauce

cooked pasta for serving

1. Place chicken in bottom of slow cooker.

2. Sprinkle seasonings over chicken.

3. Pour sauce over seasoned meat, stirring to be sure chicken is completely covered.

4. Cover. Cook on Low 6 hours or on High 3½–4 hours.

5. Serve over pasta.

Balsamic Chicken

Makes 4 servings

Hope Comerford, Clinton Township, MI

Prep. Time: 10 minutes & Cooking Time: 5–6 hours & Ideal slow-cooker size: 3-qt.

2 lbs. boneless, skinless chicken breasts

2 Tbsp. olive oil

½ tsp. salt

½ tsp. pepper

1 onion, halved and sliced

28-oz. can diced tomatoes

½ cup balsamic vinegar

2 tsp. sugar

2 tsp. garlic powder

2 tsp. Italian seasoning

cooked pasta for serving

1. Place chicken in crock. Drizzle with olive oil and sprinkle with salt and pepper.

2. Spread the onion over the top of the chicken.

3. In a bowl, mix together the diced tomatoes, balsamic vinegar, sugar, garlic powder, and Italian seasoning. Pour this over the chicken and onions.

4. Cover and cook on Low for 5–6 hours.

5. Serve over cooked pasta.

Simple Lemon Garlic Chicken

Makes 4–6 servings

Genelle Taylor, Perrysburg, OH

Prep. Time: 10 minutes ⚬ *Cooking Time: 5–6 hours* ⚬ *Ideal slow-cooker size: 5- or 6-qt.*

4–6 chicken breasts

2 tsp. minced garlic

¼ cup olive oil

1 Tbsp. parsley flakes

2 Tbsp. lemon juice (or juice of 1 whole lemon)

1. Place chicken breasts in slow cooker.

2. Combine garlic, olive oil, parsley flakes, and lemon juice; pour over chicken.

3. Cover and cook for 5–6 hours on Low.

Super Easy Chicken

Makes 4 servings

Mary Seielstad, Sparks, NV
Hope Comerford, Clinton Township, MI

Prep. Time: 5 minutes ⚓ *Cooking Time: 5–6 hours* ⚓ *Ideal slow-cooker size: 4-qt.*

4 boneless, skinless chicken breast halves

0.7 oz. pkg. dry Italian dressing mix

1 cup warm water or chicken stock

1. Place chicken in slow cooker. Sprinkle with dressing mix. Pour water around chicken.

2. Cover. Cook on Low 5–6 hours, or until juices run clear.

Shredded Lime Chicken

Makes 6 servings

Mary Seielstad, Sparks, NV
Hope Comerford, Clinton Township, MI

Prep. Time: 10 minutes ⚜ Cooking Time: 5–6 hours ⚜ Ideal slow-cooker size: 3-qt.

1½ lbs. boneless, skinless chicken breasts

2 limes, juiced

1 Tbsp. chili powder

1 tsp. salt

2 tsp. fresh minced garlic

16-oz. jar salsa of your choosing

1 small onion, chopped

1 cup frozen corn

1. Place chicken breasts in crock.

2. In a bowl, mix together the remaining ingredients. Pour this over the chicken.

3. Cover and cook on Low for 5–6 hours.

4. Remove chicken and shred between two forks. Stir back through juices in the crock.

Serving suggestion:
    This is great in tacos or on top of nachos.

Cherry Chicken

Makes 4–6 servings

Hope Comerford, Clinton Township, MI

Prep. Time: 5 minutes ⚭ *Cooking Time: 7–8 hours* ⚭ *Ideal slow-cooker size: 4-qt.*

4 chicken leg quarters

2 cups whole cherries, pitted then chopped

¼ cup sugar

I small onion, halved and sliced

I tsp. salt

I tsp. garlic powder

¼ tsp. pepper

1. Place chicken leg quarters in crock.

2. In a bowl, mix together the remaining ingredients. Pour this over the chicken in the crock.

3. Cover and cook on Low for 7–8 hours.

Apricot Chicken

Makes 4–6 servings

Hope Comerford, Clinton Township, MI

Prep. Time: 5 minutes ⚭ *Cooking Time: 7–8 hours* ⚭ *Ideal slow-cooker size: 5-qt.*

6–8 bone-in chicken thighs or legs, or combination

1.4 oz. package onion soup mix

1 cup apricot preserves or jam

½ cup chicken broth

2 Tbsp. apple cider vinegar

1 tsp. quick-cooking tapioca

1 tsp. basil

⅛ tsp. pepper

1. Place chicken in crock.

2. In a bowl, mix together the remaining ingredients. Pour over the chicken.

3. Cover and cook on Low for 7–8 hours.

Barbecued Chicken

Makes 6 servings

Charlotte Shaffer, East Earl, PA

Prep. Time: 20 minutes & Cooking Time: 6–8 hours & Ideal slow-cooker size: 3- or 4-qt.

I lb. frying chicken, cut up and skin removed (organic or free-range, if possible)

10¾-oz. can condensed tomato soup

¾ cup onion, chopped

¼ cup vinegar

3 Tbsp. brown sugar

I Tbsp. Worcestershire sauce

½ tsp. salt

¼ tsp. dried basil

1. Place chicken in slow cooker.

2. Combine all remaining ingredients and pour over chicken, making sure that the sauce glazes all the pieces.

3. Cover. Cook on Low 6–8 hours.

Sweet Barbecued Chicken

Makes 4–6 servings

Shelia Heil, Lancaster, PA

Prep. Time: 10 minutes   Cooking Time: 4–6 hours   Ideal slow-cooker size: 4-qt.

18-oz. bottle of sweet barbecue sauce
¼ cup vinegar
1 tsp. red pepper flakes
¼ cup brown sugar
1 tsp. garlic powder
4–6 chicken breasts

1. Mix all ingredients, except chicken.

2. Place chicken in crock.

3. Pour sauce mixture over chicken.

4. Cook on Low 4–6 hours.

Cranberry Onion Turkey Breast

Makes 6 servings

Gail Bush, Landenberg, PA

Prep. Time: 10 minutes ⚜ *Cooking Time: 6–8 hours* ⚜ *Ideal slow-cooker size: 5- or 6-qt.*

1 uncooked turkey breast, skin removed

15-oz. can whole-berry cranberry sauce

1 envelope low-sodium dry onion soup mix

½ cup orange juice

½ tsp. salt

¼ tsp. black pepper

1. Place turkey breast in slow cooker.

2. Combine remaining ingredients. Pour over turkey.

3. Cover. Cook on Low 6–8 hours.

Turkey Cacciatore

Makes 6 servings

Dorothy VanDeest, Memphis, TN

Prep. Time: 20 minutes   *Cooking Time: 4 hours*   *Ideal slow-cooker size: 4-qt.*

2½ cups cut-up cooked turkey

1 tsp. salt

dash pepper

1 Tbsp. dried onion flakes

1 green bell pepper, seeded and finely chopped

1 clove garlic, finely chopped

15-oz. can low-sodium whole tomatoes, mashed

4-oz. can sliced mushrooms, drained

2 tsp. tomato paste

1 bay leaf

¼ tsp. dried thyme

2 Tbsp. finely chopped pimento

1. Combine all ingredients well in slow cooker.

2. Cover. Cook on Low 4 hours. Remove bay leaf before serving.

Cheesy Stuffed Peppers

Makes 8 servings

Jean Moore, Pendleton, IN

Prep. Time: 40 minutes & Cooking Time: 3–9 hours & Ideal slow-cooker size: 4- or 6-qt. (large enough so that all peppers sit on the bottom of the cooker)

8 small green bell peppers, tops removed and seeded

10-oz. pkg. frozen corn

¾ lb. lean ground turkey

¾ lb. extra-lean ground beef

8-oz. can tomato sauce

½ tsp. garlic powder

¼ tsp. black pepper

1 cup shredded American cheese

½ tsp. Worcestershire sauce

¼ cup chopped onions

3 Tbsp. water

2 Tbsp. ketchup

1. Wash peppers and drain well. Combine all ingredients except water and ketchup in mixing bowl. Stir well.

2. Stuff peppers ⅔ full with ground meat mixture.

3. Pour water in slow cooker. Arrange peppers on top.

4. Pour ketchup over peppers.

5. Cover. Cook on High 3–4 hours or on Low 7–9 hours.

Ground Turkey Potato Dinner

Makes 6 servings

Marjorie Yoder Guengerich, Harrisonburg, VA

Prep. Time: 25 minutes ⚭ *Cooking Time: 4–8 hours* ⚭ *Ideal slow-cooker size: 4- or 5-qt.*

1 lb. ground turkey

5 cups sliced raw potatoes

1 onion, sliced

½ tsp. salt

dash black pepper

1 tsp. garlic powder

1 tsp. onion powder

14½-oz. can cut green beans, undrained

4-oz. can mushroom pieces, undrained, *optional*

10¾-oz. can cream of chicken soup

1. Crumble uncooked ground turkey into slow cooker.

2. Add potatoes, onion, salt, pepper, garlic powder, and onion powder.

3. Add beans and, if using, mushrooms. Pour soup over top.

4. Cover. Cook on High 4 hours or on Low 6–8 hours.

Turkey Meatloaf

Makes 8 servings

Martha Ann Auker, Landisburg, PA

Prep. Time: 30 minutes ❧ *Cooking Time: 4–5 hours* ❧ *Ideal slow-cooker size: 4-qt.*

1½ lbs. lean ground turkey
2 eggs
⅓ cup ketchup
1 Tbsp. Worcestershire sauce
1 tsp. dried basil
½ tsp. salt
½ tsp. black pepper
2 small onions, chopped
2 potatoes, finely shredded
2 small red bell peppers, finely chopped

1. Combine all ingredients in a large bowl.

2. Shape into a loaf to fit in your slow cooker. Place in slow cooker.

3. Cover. Cook on Low 4–5 hours.

Beef and Pork Dump Dinners

Red Wine Apple Roast

Makes 10 servings

Rose Hankins, Stevensville, MD

Prep. Time: 15 minutes ⚭ Cooking Time: 6–8 hours ⚭ Ideal slow-cooker size: 4- or 5-qt.

3-lb. eye of round beef roast

3 cups thinly sliced onions

1½ cups chopped apples, peeled or unpeeled

3 cloves garlic, chopped

1 cup red wine

salt and pepper to taste

1. Put roast in slow cooker. Layer onions, apples, and garlic on top of roast.

2. Carefully pour wine over roast without disturbing its toppings.

3. Sprinkle with salt and pepper.

4. Cover. Cook on Low 6–8 hours, or until meat is tender but not dry.

Coca-Cola Roast

Makes 6 servings

Hope Comerford, Clinton Township, MI

Prep. Time: 10 minutes ⚬ *Cooking Time: 8–10 hours* ⚬ *Ideal slow-cooker size: 6-qt.*

3–4 lb. boneless bottom round steak

5–6 small potatoes, cut if you'd like

4–5 medium-sized carrots peeled, cut in half or thirds

2–3 cloves garlic, chopped

salt to taste

pepper to taste

12-oz. can Coca-Cola

1. Place roast in crock.

2. Place potatoes and carrots around roast.

3. Sprinkle roast and veggies with the garlic, salt, and pepper.

4. Pour the can of Coca-Cola over the top.

5. Cover and cook on Low for 8–10 hours.

Texas Pot Roast

Makes 6 servings

Genelle Taylor, Perrysburg, OH

Prep. Time: 15 minutes ☙ Cooking Time: 8–10 hours ☙ Ideal slow-cooker size: 6-qt.

2–2½ lb. chuck roast

½ onion, chopped

½ bell pepper (any color), chopped

2 stalks celery, chopped

2 large potatoes, chopped into chunks, *optional*

2 cloves garlic, minced

½ cup tomato sauce

½ cup barbecue sauce

2 beef bouillon cubes

½ cup water

I tsp. salt

I tsp. black pepper

½ tsp. dried thyme

1. Place roast in slow cooker.

2. Top with vegetables and potatoes (if using).

3. In small bowl, stir together tomato sauce, barbecue sauce, boullion cubes, water, and spices. Pour over roast and vegetables.

4. Cook on Low for 8–10 hours.

Beef with Broccoli

Makes 4 servings

Genelle Taylor, Perrysburg, OH

Prep. Time: 10 minutes & Cooking Time: 5–6 hours & Ideal slow-cooker size: 5- or 6-qt.

1 cup beef broth

½ cup low-sodium soy sauce

⅓ cup brown sugar

1 Tbsp. sesame oil

3 cloves garlic, minced

1½ lb. boneless beef chuck roast or steak, sliced into thin strips

2 Tbsp. cornstarch

14-oz. bag frozen broccoli florets

1. In a mixing bowl, whisk together the beef broth, soy sauce, brown sugar, sesame oil, and garlic.

2. Lay the beef strips in the slow cooker and pour the sauce over, tossing the strips to coat.

3. Cover and cook on Low for 5–6 hours

4. Remove 4 Tbsp. of the sauce and whisk it in a small bowl with cornstarch. Slowly stir this into slow cooker.

5. Add broccoli. Cook an additional 30 minutes.

Serving suggestion:
 Serve over white or brown rice.

Pepper Steak

Makes 4–6 servings

Genelle Taylor, Perrysburg, OH

Prep. Time: 15 minutes & Cooking Time: 4–6 hours & Ideal slow-cooker size: 5- or 6-qt.

2 lbs. top sirloin, cut into 2-inch strips

I yellow onion, diced

I 14½-oz. can sliced stewed tomatoes

2 Tbsp. brown sugar

3 Tbsp. soy sauce

I Tbsp. Worcestershire sauce

¾ cup chopped green bell pepper

I cup beef broth

I tsp. minced garlic

¼ tsp. ground cayenne pepper

¼ tsp. ground ginger

½ tsp. seasoned salt

¼ tsp. black pepper

3 Tbsp. cornstarch

3 Tbsp. water

I red bell pepper, thinly sliced

I yellow bell pepper, thinly sliced

I orange bell pepper, thinly sliced

1. Place steak and onion in slow cooker.

2. Pour in tomatoes, brown sugar, soy sauce, Worcestershire sauce, green pepper, beef broth, minced garlic, cayenne pepper, ginger, seasoned salt, and pepper.

3. In a small bowl, whisk cornstarch and water together; stir into slow cooker.

4. Cover and cook on Low for 4–6 hours.

5. About 2 hours before you are ready to eat, add in thinly sliced red, yellow, and orange peppers. Stir and cover again. Complete last 2 hours of cooking.

Serving suggestion:
Serve over rice or quinoa.

Mexicali Round Steak

Makes 6 servings

Marcia S. Myer, Manheim, PA

Prep. Time: 20 minutes ♣ Cooking Time: 5–6 hours ♣ Ideal slow-cooker size: 5-qt.

1½ lbs. round steak

1 cup frozen corn, thawed

½–1 cup fresh cilantro, chopped, according to your taste preference

½ cup beef broth

3 ribs celery, sliced

1 large onion, sliced

20-oz. jar salsa

15-oz. can black beans, or pinto beans, rinsed and drained

1 cup grated cheddar cheese

1. Cut beef into 6 pieces. Place in slow cooker.

2. Combine remaining ingredients except cheese, and pour over beef.

3. Cover. Cook on Low 5–6 hours.

4. Sprinkle with cheese before serving.

Beef Stroganoff

Makes 6 servings

Gloria Julien, Gladstone, MI

Prep. Time: 15 minutes & Cooking Time: 3½–4½ hours & Ideal slow-cooker size: 4-qt.

1½ lbs. lean beef stewing meat, trimmed of fat
1 onion, chopped
1 clove garlic, minced
1 tsp. salt
¼ tsp. black pepper
1 lb. fresh mushrooms
10¾-oz. can cream of mushroom soup
1 cup water
1 cup sour cream

1. Combine all ingredients except sour cream in slow cooker.

2. Cook on Low 3–4 hours.

3. Stir in sour cream.

4. Cook on High for a few minutes to heat sour cream.

Beef Pitas

Makes 2 servings

Dede Peterson, Rapid City, SD

Prep. Time: 15 minutes ⚜ *Cooking Time: 2–3 hours* ⚜ *Ideal slow-cooker size: 2-qt.*

½ lb. beef or pork, cut into small cubes

½ tsp. dried oregano

dash black pepper

1 cup chopped fresh tomatoes

2 Tbsp. diced fresh green bell peppers

¼ cup sour cream

1 tsp. red wine vinegar

1 tsp. olive oil

2 large pita breads, heated and cut in half

1. Place meat in slow cooker. Sprinkle with oregano and black pepper.

2. Cook on Low 2–3 hours.

3. In a separate bowl, combine tomatoes, green peppers, sour cream, vinegar, and oil.

4. Fill pitas with meat. Top with vegetable–sour cream mixture.

Flavorful French Dip

Makes 8 servings

Marcella Stalter, Flanagan, IL

Prep. Time: 5 minutes ⚘ *Cooking Time: 5–6 hours* ⚘ *Ideal slow-cooker size: 3½-qt.*

3-lb. chuck roast
2 cups water
½ cup soy sauce
1 tsp. dried rosemary
1 tsp. dried thyme
1 tsp. garlic powder
1 bay leaf
3–4 whole peppercorns

1. Place roast in slow cooker. Add water, soy sauce, and seasonings.

2. Cover. Cook on High 5–6 hours, or until beef is tender.

3. Remove beef from broth. Shred with fork. Keep warm.

4. Strain broth. Skim fat. Pour broth into small cups for dipping.

Serving suggestion:

Serve beef on French rolls.

NOTE
If you have leftover broth, freeze it to use it later for gravy or as a soup base.

German Dinner

Makes 6 servings

Sharon Miller, Holmesville, OH

Prep. Time: 15 minutes ⚬ *Cooking Time: 7–8 hours* ⚬ *Ideal slow-cooker size: 4- or 5-qt.*

32-oz. bag sauerkraut, drained
1 lb. extra-lean ground beef
1 small green bell pepper, grated
2 11½-oz. cans V8 juice
½ cup diced potatoes
½ cup chopped celery, *optional*

1. Combine all ingredients in slow cooker.

2. Cook for 7–8 hours, or until potatoes are tender.

Steak and Rice Dinner

Makes 8 servings

Susan Scheel, West Fargo, ND

Prep. Time: 15–20 minutes & *Cooking Time: 4–6 hours* & *Ideal slow-cooker size: 5-qt.*

I cup uncooked wild rice, rinsed and drained

I cup chopped celery

I cup chopped carrots

2 4-oz. cans mushrooms, drained

I large onion, chopped

½ cup slivered almonds

3 beef bouillon cubes

2½ tsp. seasoned salt

2 lbs. boneless round steak, cut in bite-sized pieces

3 cups water

1. Layer ingredients in slow cooker in order listed. Do not stir.

2. Cover. Cook on Low 4–6 hours.

3. Stir before serving.

Chili-Lime Mexican Shredded Beef

Makes 6–8 servings

Genelle Taylor, Perrysburg, OH

Prep. Time: 10 minutes ⚹ Cooking Time: 8 hours ⚹ Ideal slow-cooker size: 5- to 6-qt.

2–3-lb. beef chuck roast
4 cups lemon-lime soda
1 tsp. chili powder
1 tsp. salt
3 cloves garlic, crushed
2 limes, juiced

1. Place the roast in slow cooker.

2. Pour soda over roast.

3. Season with chili powder, salt, and garlic.

4. Cover and cook on Low for 8 hours.

5. Shred the beef, return to crock, pour lime juice over, and stir.

Serving suggestion:
  Serve hot, with black beans and rice, or use in tacos.

Low-Cal Meatloaf

Makes 6 servings

Jeanette Oberholtzer, Manheim, PA; Charlotte Shaffer, East Earl, PA; Dorothy VanDeest, Memphis, TN

Prep. Time: 25 minutes & Cooking Time: 4–5 hours & Ideal slow-cooker size: 3½-qt.

½ lb. extra-lean ground beef
3 cups shredded cabbage
I green bell pepper, chopped
½ tsp. salt
I Tbsp. dried onion flakes
½ tsp. caraway seeds, *optional*

1. Thoroughly combine all ingredients.

2. Shape into a round loaf.

3. Place on rack in slow cooker.

4. Cover. Cook on Low 4–5 hours.

Extra Flavorful Meatloaf

Makes 6 servings

Karen Waggoner, Joplin, MO

Prep. Time: 20–30 minutes ♣ *Cooking Time: 4½ hours* ♣ *Ideal slow-cooker size: 4-qt.*

1¼ lbs. extra-lean ground beef

4 cups hash browns, thawed

1 egg, lightly beaten

2 Tbsp. dry vegetable soup mix

2 Tbsp. low-sodium taco seasoning

2 cups shredded cheddar cheese, *divided*

1. Mix together ground beef, hash browns, egg, soup mix, taco seasoning, and 1 cup of cheese. Shape into loaf.

2. Line slow cooker with tin foil, allowing ends of foil to extend out over edges of cooker, enough to grab hold of and to lift the loaf out when it's finished cooking. Spray the foil with nonfat cooking spray.

3. Place loaf in cooker. Cover. Cook on Low 4 hours.

4. Sprinkle with remaining cheese and cover until melted.

5. Gently lift loaf out, using tin-foil handles. Allow to rest 10 minutes, then slice and serve.

Pork and Beef Barbecue for Sandwiches

Makes 14 servings

Susan Scheel, West Fargo, ND

Prep. Time: 25 minutes ♣ Cooking Time: 3–4 hours ♣ Ideal slow-cooker size: 5- or 6-qt.

8-oz. can tomato sauce

½ cup brown sugar, packed

¼ cup chili powder, or less

¼ cup cider vinegar

2 tsp. Worcestershire sauce

1 tsp. salt

1 lb. lean beef stewing meat, cut into ¾-inch cubes

1 lb. lean pork tenderloin, cut into ¾-inch cubes

3 green bell peppers, chopped

hamburger buns

3 large onions, chopped

1. Combine tomato sauce, brown sugar, chili powder, cider vinegar, Worcestershire sauce, and salt in slow cooker.

2. Stir in meats, green peppers, and onions.

3. Cover. Cook on High 3–4 hours.

4. Shred meat with two forks. Stir all ingredients together well.

5. Serve on buns.

Barbecued Pork

Makes 8 servings

Rhonda L. Burgoon, Collingswood, NJ

Prep. Time: 15 minutes ♣ Cooking Time: 4 hours ♣ Ideal slow-cooker size: 4- or 5-qt.

2 lbs. boneless pork top loin

1½ cups onions, chopped

1 cup cola

1 cup of your favorite barbecue sauce

wheat or multigrain buns

1. Place pork in slow cooker. Combine all other ingredients except buns in a bowl and then pour over pork.

2. Cover. Cook on High 4 hours or until meat is very tender.

3. Slice or shred pork. Stir back into sauce.

4. Serve on wheat or multigrain buns.

Country Barbecued Ribs

Makes 10 servings

Mary Longenecker, Bethel, PA

Prep. Time: 10–15 minutes ❧ *Cooking Time: 8–10 hours* ❧ *Ideal slow-cooker size: 4-qt.*

3 lbs. lean country-style ribs

2½ lbs. sauerkraut, rinsed

2 cups of your favorite barbecue sauce

1 cup water

1. Place ribs on bottom of cooker.

2. Layer sauerkraut over ribs.

3. Mix barbecue sauce and water together. Pour over meat and kraut.

4. Cover. Cook on Low 8–10 hours.

Barbecued Pork Chops

Makes 6 servings

Loretta Weisz, Auburn, WA

Prep. Time: 10 minutes ⚜ *Cooking Time: 5–6 hours* ⚜ *Ideal slow-cooker size: 5-qt.*

4 loin pork chops, ¾-inch thick

1 cup ketchup

1 cup hot water

2 Tbsp. vinegar

1 Tbsp. Worcestershire sauce

2 tsp. brown sugar

½ tsp. black pepper

½ tsp. chili powder

½ tsp. paprika

1. Place pork chops in slow cooker.

2. Combine remaining ingredients. Pour over chops.

3. Cover. Cook on High 5–6 hours, or until tender but not dry.

4. Cut chops in half and serve.

Easy Sweet-and-Sour Pork Chops

Makes 6 servings

Jeanne Hertzog, Bethlehem, PA

Prep. Time: 5 minutes ♣ *Cooking Time: 7–8 hours* ♣ *Ideal slow-cooker size: 4-qt.*

16-oz. bag frozen stir-fry vegetables
6 bone-in pork chops
12-oz. bottle sweet-and-sour sauce
½ cup water
1 cup frozen snow peas

1. Place stir-fry vegetables in slow cooker. Arrange chops on top.

2. Combine sauce and water. Pour over chops.

3. Cover. Cook on Low 7–8 hours.

4. Turn to High and add snow peas.

5. Cover. Cook on High 5 minutes.

Golden Mushroom Pork Chops with Apples

Makes 4–6 servings

Hope Comerford, Clinton Township, MI

Prep. Time: 10 minutes   ⚖   Cooking Time: 8–9 hours   ⚖   Ideal slow-cooker size: 5-qt.

2 10½-oz. cans condensed golden mushroom soup

½ cup chicken stock

1 Tbsp. brown sugar

1 Tbsp. Worcestershire sauce

1 tsp. crushed dried thyme leaves

4 large Granny Smith apples, peeled and sliced

2 large onions, halved and sliced

2 lbs. boneless pork chops

1. In the crock, mix the soup, chicken stock, brown sugar, Worcestershire, and thyme.

2. Add apples, onions, and pork. Toss together.

3. Cook on Low 8–9 hours.

Pork Chops and Mushrooms

Makes 4 servings

Michele Ruvola, Selden, NY

Prep. Time: 5 minutes ⚜ *Cooking Time: 6–8 hours* ⚜ *Ideal slow-cooker size: 4- to 5-qt.*

4 boneless pork chops, ½-inch thick

2 medium onions, sliced

1 cup sliced mushrooms

1 envelope dry onion soup mix

¼ cup water

10¾-oz. can golden cream of mushroom soup

1. Place pork chops in greased slow cooker. Top with onions and mushrooms.

2. Combine soup mix, water, and mushroom soup. Pour over mushrooms.

3. Cover. Cook on Low 6–8 hours.

Quick Italian Chops

Makes 2–4 servings

Jan Moore, Wellsville, KS

Prep. Time: 5 minutes   *Cooking Time: 2–4 hours*   *Ideal slow-cooker size: 3½- to 4-qt.*

16-oz. bottle Italian salad dressing (use
less if cooking only 2 chops)
2–4 pork chops

1. Place pork chops in slow cooker. Pour salad dressing over chops.

2. Cover. Cook on Low 2–4 hours, or until tender.

Variation:

Add cubed potatoes and thinly sliced carrots and onions to meat before pouring dressing over top.

Applesauce Pork Chops

Makes 4 servings

Hope Comerford, Clinton Township, MI

Prep. Time: 5 minutes & Cooking Time: 7 hours & Ideal slow-cooker size: 4-qt.

2 lbs. thick-cut bone-in pork chops

1 ½ cups natural applesauce

¼ cup brown sugar

1–2 Tbsp. minced onion

1 tsp. salt

¼ tsp. pepper

1. Place pork chops in crock.

2. In a bowl, mix together the remaining ingredients. Pour this over the pork chops.

3. Cover and cook on Low for 7 hours.

Cranberry Pork Tenderloin

Makes 8 servings

Janice Yoskovich, Carmichaels, PA

Prep. Time: 10 minutes   ❧   Cooking Time: 4 hours   ❧   Ideal slow-cooker size: 4-qt.

1½ lbs. pork tenderloin
12 oz. chili sauce
16-oz. can jellied cranberry sauce
2 Tbsp. brown sugar
5 cups cooked long-grain enriched rice

1. Place pork tenderloin in slow cooker.

2. Mix together chili sauce, cranberry sauce, and brown sugar. Pour over pork.

3. Cover and cook on Low 4 hours, or until cooked through but not dry.

4. Serve over rice.

Salsa Verde Pork

Makes 6 servings

Hope Comerford, Clinton Township, MI

Prep. Time: 20 minutes & *Cooking Time: 6–6½ hours* & *Ideal slow-cooker size: 4-qt.*

1½-lb. boneless pork loin
1 large sweet onion, halved and sliced
2 large tomatoes, chopped
16-oz. jar salsa verde (green salsa)
½ cup dry white wine
4 cloves garlic, minced
1 tsp. cumin
½ tsp. chili powder

1. Place the pork loin in the crock and add the rest of the ingredients on top.

2. Cover and cook on Low for 6–6½ hours.

3. Break apart the pork with two forks and mix with contents of crock.

Serving suggestion:

Serve over cooked brown rice or quinoa.

Cranberry Jalapeño Pork Roast

Makes 4–6 servings

Hope Comerford, Clinton Township, MI

Prep. Time: 10 minutes ⚹ Cooking Time: 7–8 hours ⚹ Ideal slow-cooker size: 3-qt.

2–3-lb. pork roast
1 tsp. garlic powder
½ tsp. salt
½ tsp. pepper
1 small onion, chopped
½ jalapeño, seeded and diced
14-oz. can jellied cranberry sauce

1. Place pork roast in crock.

2. Season the pork roast with the garlic powder, salt, and pepper.

3. Dump in the onion and jalapeño.

4. Spoon the jellied cranberry sauce over the top of the contents of the crock.

5. Cover and cook on Low for 7–8 hours.

Zesty Pork Burritos

Makes 8–10 servings

Hope Comerford, Clinton Township, MI

Prep. Time: 5 minutes ⚬ *Cooking Time: 8–10 hours* ⚬ *Ideal slow-cooker size: 3-qt.*

3–4-lb. pork shoulder

14½-oz. can diced tomatoes with green chilies

1-oz. pkg. low-sodium taco seasoning

2 tsp. honey

flour tortillas

Optional burrito fixings:

shredded cheese, lettuce, sour cream, refried beans . . . anything you want!

1. Place all ingredients in crock (except tortillas and optional fixings).

2. Cover and cook on Low 8–10 hours.

3. Remove pork and shred it between two forks. Stir it back through the juices.

4. Serve in tortillas with optional toppings, rolled up as burritos.

One-Pot German Dinner

Makes 6–8 servings

Donna Treloar, Muncie, IN

Prep. Time: 15–30 minutes ⚬ *Cooking Time: 7 hours* ⚬ *Ideal slow-cooker size: 4-qt.*

8–10 cups shredded fresh cabbage

3 potatoes, peeled and cubed

1 large onion, chopped

dash salt

dash pepper

14½-oz. can chicken broth

2 lbs. kielbasa, or sausage of your choice, cut into serving-sized pieces

1. Combine cabbage, potatoes, onion, salt, and pepper in slow cooker.

2. Add chicken broth.

3. Place sausage pieces on top.

4. Cover and cook on Low 7 hours, or until vegetables are tender.

Beer-Poached Italian Sausage

Makes 4–5 servings

Hope Comerford, Clinton Township, MI

Prep. Time: 5 minutes ⚬ *Cooking Time: 6–7 hours* ⚬ *Ideal slow-cooker size: 3-qt.*

1 lb. sweet Italian sausage

12 oz. beer of your choice

hot dog buns

1. Place the Italian sausage in crock and pour the beer over the top.

2. Cover and cook on Low for 6–7 hours.

3. Serve in the hot dog buns with toppings of your choice.

Cabbage with Kielbasa

Makes 8 servings

Millie Schellenburg, Washington, NJ

Prep. Time: 20–30 minutes ⚜ *Cooking Time: 3–4 hours* ⚜ *Ideal slow-cooker size: 6-qt.*

2 cups water

1½ medium-sized heads of cabbage, chopped

¾ lb. kielbasa, cut into ½-inch slices

8 medium-sized potatoes, cut into chunks

1 onion, sliced

1. Combine all ingredients in slow cooker.

2. Cover. Cook on Low 3–4 hours, or until cabbage and potatoes are done to your liking.

Ham & Yam Dish

Makes 8 servings

Leona Miller, Millersburg, OH

Prep. Time: 15 minutes & Cooking Time: 1½–4 hours & Ideal slow-cooker size: 4- or 5-qt.

40-oz. can yams in water, drained

1 ½ lbs. extra-lean smoked ham, cut into bite-sized cubes

20-oz. can unsweetened pineapple chunks, or crushed pineapple, in light juice, drained

¼ cup dark brown sugar

1. Spray slow cooker with nonfat cooking spray.

2. Stir all ingredients together gently in the slow cooker.

3. Cook on High 1½–2 hours or on Low 3–4 hours.

Meatless and Pasta Dump Dinners

Crustless Spinach Quiche

Makes 8 servings

Barbara Hoover, Landisville, PA

Prep. Time: 15 minutes ⚗ Cooking Time: 2–4 hours ⚗ Ideal slow-cooker size: 3- or 4-qt.

2 10-oz. pkgs. frozen chopped spinach

2 cups cottage cheese

4 Tbsp. (½ stick) butter, cut into pieces

1½ cups sharp cheese, cubed

3 eggs, beaten

¼ cup flour

1 tsp. salt

1. Grease interior of slow cooker crock.

2. Thaw spinach completely. Squeeze as dry as you can. Then place in crock.

3. Stir in all other ingredients and combine well.

4. Cover. Cook on Low 2–4 hours, or until quiche is set. Stick blade of knife into center of quiche. If blade comes out clean, quiche is set. If it doesn't, cover and cook another 15 minutes or so.

5. When cooked, allow to stand 10–15 minutes so mixture can firm up. Then serve.

Variations:

1. Double the recipe if you wish. Cook it in a 5-qt. slow cooker.

2. Omit cottage cheese. Add 1 cup milk, 1 tsp. baking powder, and increase flour to 1 cup instead.

3. Reserve sharp cheese and sprinkle on top. Allow to melt before serving.

—Barbara Jean Fabel

Zucchini Casserole

Makes 8 servings

Mary Clair Wenger, Kimmswick, MO

Prep. Time: 25 minutes ♣ Cooking Time: 4–5 hours ♣ Ideal slow-cooker size: 4-qt.

5 cups diced zucchini
1 cup grated carrots
1 small onion, diced finely
1½ cups biscuit baking mix
½ cup grated Parmesan cheese
4 eggs, beaten
¼ cup olive oil
2 tsp. dried marjoram
½ tsp. salt
pepper to taste

1. Mix together all ingredients. Pour into greased slow cooker.

2. Cover and cook on Low for 4–5 hours, until set. Remove lid last 30 minutes to allow excess moisture to evaporate.

3. Serve hot or room temperature.

Thai Veggie Curry

Makes 4–5 servings

Christen Chew, Lancaster, PA

Prep. Time: 30 minutes   Cooking Time: 5–6 hours   Ideal slow-cooker size: 4- or 5-qt.

2 large carrots, thinly sliced

1 medium onion, chopped

3 cloves garlic, chopped

2 large potatoes, peeled or not, diced

15½-oz. can garbanzo beans, rinsed and drained

14½-oz. can diced tomatoes, undrained

2 Tbsp. curry powder

1 tsp. ground coriander

1 tsp. cayenne pepper

2 cups vegetable stock

½ cup frozen green peas

½ cup coconut milk

salt to taste

cooked rice

1. Grease interior of slow cooker crock.

2. Stir all ingredients except peas, coconut milk, salt, and cooked rice into crock. Mix together well, making sure seasonings are distributed throughout.

3. Cover. Cook on Low 5–6 hours, or until vegetables are as tender as you like them.

4. Just before serving, stir in peas and coconut milk. Season with salt to taste.

5. Serve over cooked rice.

Herbed Rice and Lentil Bake

Makes 4 servings

Peg Zannotti, Tulsa, OK

Prep. Time: 15 minutes & Cooking Time: 2–4 hours & Ideal slow-cooker size: 4-qt.

2⅔ cups vegetable broth or water

¾ cup dried green lentils, picked over for any stones and rinsed

¾ cup chopped onions

½ cup uncooked brown rice

¼ cup dry white wine or water

½ tsp. dried basil

¼ tsp. dried oregano

¼ tsp. dried thyme

⅛ tsp. garlic powder

½ cup shredded Italian-mix cheese or cheddar cheese

1. Grease interior of slow cooker crock.

2. Place everything in the crock, except cheese. Stir together until well mixed.

3. Cover. Cook on Low 3–4 hours, or on High 2–3 hours, or until lentils and rice are both as tender as you like them.

4. Just before serving, sprinkle top with cheese. Allow to melt, and then serve.

Variations:

1. Add ½ tsp. salt in Step 2 if you wish.

2. Before adding cheese, top mixture with ½ cup Italian-flavored panko bread crumbs. Cook, uncovered, 5–10 minutes. Sprinkle with cheese. Allow cheese to melt, and then serve.

Barbecued Lentils

Makes 8 servings

Sue Hamilton, Benson, AZ

Prep. Time: 5 minutes ❧ *Cooking Time: 6–8 hours* ❧ *Ideal slow-cooker size: 4-qt.*

2 cups barbecue sauce
3½ cups water
1 lb. dry lentils
1 pkg. vegetarian hot dogs, sliced

1. Combine all ingredients in slow cooker.

2. Cover. Cook on Low 6–8 hours.

Italian Vegetable Pasta Sauce

Makes 4–6 servings

Patti Boston, Newark, OH

Prep. Time: 15 minutes ❧ *Cooking Time: 4½–9 hours* ❧ *Ideal slow-cooker size: 2½-qt.*

3 small carrots, sliced

1 small onion, chopped

2 small potatoes, diced

2 Tbsp. chopped parsley

1 garlic clove, minced

1¼ tsp. dried basil

½ tsp. salt

¼ tsp. pepper

16-oz. can red kidney beans, undrained

3 cups vegetable broth

14½-oz. can stewed tomatoes, with juice

1. Layer carrots, onion, potatoes, parsley, garlic, basil, salt, pepper, and kidney beans in slow cooker.

2. Add vegetable broth and stewed tomatoes.

3. Cover. Cook on Low 8–9 hours, or on High 4½–5½ hours, until vegetables are tender.

Slow Cooker Baked Ziti

Makes 4–6 servings

Hope Comerford, Clinton Township, MI

Prep. Time: 10 minutes ⚜ *Cooking Time: 4 hours* ⚜ *Ideal slow-cooker size: 3-qt.*

28-oz. can crushed tomatoes

15-oz. can tomato sauce

1½ tsp. Italian seasoning

1 tsp. garlic powder

1 tsp. onion powder

1 tsp. pepper

1 tsp. salt

1 lb. ziti or rigatoni pasta, uncooked, *divided*

2 cups shredded mozzarella cheese, *divided*

1. Spray crock with nonstick spray.

2. In a bowl, mix together the crushed tomatoes, tomato sauce, Italian seasoning, garlic powder, onion powder, pepper, and salt.

3. In the bottom of the crock, pour ⅓ of the pasta sauce.

4. Add ½ of the pasta on top of the sauce in the crock, followed by 1 cup of the mozzarella cheese.

5. Add the rest of the pasta, the remaining pasta sauce, and the rest of the cheese.

6. Cover and cook on Low for 4 hours.

Tortellini with Broccoli

Makes 4 servings

Susan Kasting, Jenks, OK

Prep. Time: 10 minutes ❀ *Cooking Time: 2½–3 hours* ❀ *Ideal slow-cooker size: 4-qt.*

½ cup water

26-oz. jar your favorite pasta sauce, *divided*

1 Tbsp. Italian seasoning

9-oz. pkg. frozen spinach and cheese tortellini

16-oz. pkg. frozen broccoli florets

1. In a bowl, mix water, pasta sauce, and seasoning together.

2. Pour ⅓ of sauce into bottom of slow cooker. Top with all the tortellini.

3. Pour ⅓ of sauce over tortellini. Top with broccoli.

4. Pour remaining sauce over broccoli.

5. Cook on High 2½–3 hours, or until broccoli and pasta are tender but not mushy.

Cheese Tortellini and Meatballs with Vodka & Pasta Sauce

Makes 4–6 servings

Phyllis Good, Lancaster, PA

Prep. Time: 10 minutes i ⅋ Cooking Time: 6 hours ⅋ Ideal slow-cooker size: 5-qt.

1½-lb. bag frozen cheese tortellini

1½-lb. bag frozen Italian-style meatballs

20-oz. jar vodka pasta sauce

8-oz. can tomato sauce

1 cup water

½ tsp. red pepper flakes, or less if you want

1½ tsp. dried oregano

1½ tsp. dried basil

2 cups grated mozzarella cheese

1. Combine all ingredients except cheese in a greased slow cooker.

2. Cook on Low for 6 hours.

3. Top each individual serving with grated cheese.

Creamy Macaroni Dinner

Makes 6 servings

Anna Musser, Manheim, PA

Prep. Time: 7 minutes   ♣   *Cooking Time: 2½–3 hours*   ♣   *Ideal slow-cooker size: 5-qt.*

2 cups shredded cheese, your choice

2 cups macaroni, uncooked

3 cups milk

2 10¾-oz. cans cream of mushroom soup

2 cups cooked ham, or sliced hot dogs, or cooked, cubed chicken, or cooked ground beef

1. Place all ingredients in slow cooker. Mix together gently, but until well blended.

2. Cover and cook on High 2½–3 hours, or until macaroni is cooked but not overdone.

Macaroni and Velveeta Cheese

Makes 6 servings

Lisa F. Good, Harrisonburg, VA

Prep. Time: 10 minutes ⚬ Cooking Time: 2–3 hours ⚬ Ideal slow-cooker size: 2- or 3-qt.

1½ cups dry macaroni

1 Tbsp. butter

1 tsp. salt

½ lb. Velveeta Light cheese, sliced

4 cups milk

1. Combine macaroni, butter, and salt.

2. Layer cheese over top.

3. Pour in milk.

4. Cover. Cook on High 2–3 hours, or until macaroni are soft.

Extra-Cheesy Macaroni and Cheese

Makes 4 servings

Linda Thomas, Sayner, WI

Prep. Time: 10 minutes ♣ Cooking Time: 2–2½ hours ♣ Ideal slow-cooker size: 4-qt.

½ cup sour cream

10½-oz. can cheddar cheese soup

1 cup milk

3 eggs, slightly beaten

½ tsp. salt

½ tsp. coarsely ground black pepper

½ tsp. dry mustard

1½ cups uncooked elbow macaroni

2½ cups shredded sharp cheddar cheese

1. Grease interior of slow cooker crock.

2. Mix together sour cream, cheddar cheese soup, milk, eggs, salt, pepper, and dry mustard.

3. Stir in uncooked macaroni and shredded cheese.

4. Cover. Cook on Low for 2–2½ hours, until macaroni is soft and set.

5. If there's water at the edges that you don't like, turn cooker to High and cook uncovered another 15–20 minutes.

Jambalaya

Makes 5–6 servings

Doris M. Coyle-Zipp, South Ozone Park, NY

Prep. Time: 15 minutes ❧ Cooking Time: 2¼–3¾ hours ❧ Ideal slow-cooker size: 5-qt.

3½–4-lb. roasting chicken, cut up
3 onions, diced
1 carrot, sliced
3–4 cloves garlic, minced
1 tsp. dried oregano
1 tsp. dried basil
1 tsp. salt
⅛ tsp. white pepper
14-oz. can crushed tomatoes
1 lb. shelled raw shrimp
2 cups cooked rice

1. Combine all ingredients except shrimp and rice in slow cooker.

2. Cover. Cook on Low 2–3½ hours, or until chicken is tender.

3. Add shrimp and rice.

4. Cover. Cook on High 15–20 minutes, or until shrimp are done.

Simple Tuna Delight

Makes 3 servings

Karen Waggoner, Joplin, MO

Prep. Time: 5–10 minutes ⚜ *Cooking Time: 1½ hours* ⚜ *Ideal slow-cooker size: 2-qt.*

1¾ cups frozen vegetables

12-oz. can water-packed tuna, drained

10¾-oz. can condensed cream of chicken or celery soup

cooked rice or noodles

1. Combine all ingredients in slow cooker.

2. Cover. Cook on High 1½ hours, stirring occasionally.

3. Serve over hot cooked rice or noodles.

Hot Tuna Macaroni Casserole

Makes 6 servings

Dorothy VanDeest, Memphis, TN

Prep. Time: 15 minutes ❧ Cooking Time: 2–6 hours ❧ Ideal slow-cooker size: 3-qt.

2 6-oz. cans water-packed tuna, rinsed and drained

1½ cups cooked macaroni

½ cup finely chopped onions

¼ cup finely chopped green bell peppers

4-oz. can sliced mushrooms, drained

10-oz. pkg. frozen cauliflower, partially thawed

½ cup low sodium, fat-free chicken broth

1. Combine all ingredients in slow cooker. Stir well.

2. Cover. Cook on Low 4–6 hours or on High 2–3 hours.

Chocolate, Peanut Butter & More Dump Desserts

Chocolate Pudding Cake

Makes 10–12 servings

Lee Ann Hazlett, Freeport, IL I
Della Yoder, Kalona, IA

Prep. Time: 5–10 minutes ⚶ Cooking Time: 3–7 hours ⚶ Ideal slow-cooker size: 4-qt.

18½-oz. box chocolate cake mix

3.9-oz. box instant chocolate pudding mix

2 cups (16 oz.) sour cream

4 eggs

1 cup water

¾ cup oil

1 cup semisweet chocolate chips

1. Combine cake mix, pudding mix, sour cream, eggs, water, and oil in electric mixer bowl. Beat on medium speed for 2 minutes. Stir in chocolate chips.

2. Pour into greased slow cooker. Cover and cook on Low 6–7 hours, or on High 3–4 hours, or until toothpick inserted near center comes out with moist crumbs

Oh My Chocolate Dessert

Makes 8 servings

Sue Hamilton, Benson, AZ

Prep. Time: 10 minutes   Cooking Time: 3 hours   Ideal slow-cooker size: 7-qt.

48 oz. chocolate ice cream with fudge and peanut butter cups, softened

18-oz. box brownie mix

8 Tbsp. (1 stick) butter, cold

1. Spray the crock with cooking spray.

2. Spread the ice cream in the bottom of the pot.

3. Sprinkle the brownie mix on top.

4. Slice the butter into small pieces and place on top of the mix.

5. Cover and cook on High for 3 hours.

6. Remove lid and let cool 15 minutes. Serve warm or chilled.

Fudge Swirl Dump Cake

Makes 8–10 servings

Hope Comerford, Clinton Township, MI

Prep. Time: 10 minutes ⚜ *Cooking Time: 2–3 hours* ⚜ *Ideal slow-cooker size: 4- or 5-qt.*

2½ cups of a 18½-oz. box chocolate fudge cake mix

2 eggs

¾ cup water

3 Tbsp. unsweetened applesauce

¼ cup warm water

3 Tbsp. sugar

¼ cup dark chocolate chips

⅓ cup chocolate fudge sauce

1. Spray crock with nonstick spray.

2. In a bowl, mix together the first six ingredients. Pour this batter into the crock, then sprinkle the chocolate chips over the top.

3. Using a spoon, swirl the chocolate fudge sauce through the batter.

4. Cover and cook on Low for 2–3 hours.

Quick Chocolate Fudge Dump Cake

Makes 10–12 servings

Phyllis Good, Lancaster, PA

Prep. Time: 15 minutes ❧ Cooking Time: 2½–3½ hours ❧ Ideal slow-cooker size: 5-qt.

18¼-oz. box chocolate fudge cake mix,
or German chocolate cake mix

2 eggs

21-oz. can cherry pie filling

1 tsp. vanilla or almond extract, *optional*

1. Grease and flour interior of slow cooker crock.

2. In a good-sized bowl, mix together dry cake mix, eggs, pie filling, and extract if you wish. Batter will be pretty stiff.

3. Spoon into greased and floured crock.

4. Cover with slow cooker lid.

5. Bake on High 2½–3½ hours, or until tester inserted into center of cake comes out clean.

6. Remove crock from cooker and allow to cool, uncovered.

7. Serve from crock, either in wedges or spoonfuls.

Chocolate Cherry Dessert

Makes 6 servings

Janie Steele, Moore, OK

Prep. Time: 5 minutes ❧ Cooking Time: 3 hours ❧ Ideal slow-cooker size: 3-qt.

1 12½-oz. can cherry pie filling
1 box chocolate cake mix
4 Tbsp. (½ stick) butter melted
1 tsp. cinnamon

1. Pour pie filling in greased slow cooker.

2. Mix dry cake mix and melted butter together. Sprinkle this over pie filling.

3. Cover and cook on Low for 3 hours.

Serving Suggestion:
Serve with ice cream or whipped topping.

Dark Chocolate Cherry Yum

Makes 8 servings

Susan Kasting, Jenks, OK

Prep. Time: 5 minutes & *Cooking Time: 2 hours* & *Ideal slow-cooker size: 5-qt.*

2 21-oz. cans cherry pie filling
15¼-oz. box dark chocolate cake mix
8 Tbsp. (1 stick) butter, melted

1. Pour cans of pie filling into greased slow cooker.

2. Sprinkle cake mix evenly over pie filling.

3. Pour butter on top of cake mix.

4. Cook on Low for 2 hours.

Black Forest Spoon Dessert

Makes 6 servings

Marla Folkerts, Batavia, IL

Prep. Time: 10 minutes   ♒   Cooking Time: 2–2¼ hours   ♒   Ideal slow-cooker size: 4-qt.

21-oz. can cherry pie filling

18¼-oz. box chocolate cake mix

1. Preheat the slow cooker on High for 10 minutes.

2. Spray the slow cooker with cooking spray.

3. In the slow cooker, stir together the pie filling and cake mix until there is no dry cake mix visible. The batter will be a very thick and lumpy.

4. Place a paper towel on top of the slow cooker.

5. Put the slow cooker lid on the paper towel.

6. Cook on High for 2–2¼ hours or until knife inserted in the center comes out clean.

7. Serve directly from the slow cooker. Do not invert this cake.

S'mores Lava Cake

Makes 8 servings

Jennifer Freed, Rockingham, VA

Prep. Time: 10 minutes ❧ Cooking Time: 2½–3 hours ❧ Ideal slow-cooker size: 5- or 6-qt.

15¼-oz. box chocolate cake mix, plus ingredients listed on back

3.9-oz. box instant chocolate pudding mix

2 cups cold milk

½ cup mini marshmallows

¼ cup crushed graham crackers

½ cup chocolate chips

1. Grease crock.

2. Prepare cake batter according to package directions directly in crock.

3. In a bowl, prepare the chocolate pudding mix with the 2 cups of milk.

4. Cover cake mix with mini marshmallows in crock, then carefully spread pudding mix over the marshmallows.

5. Top evenly with graham crackers crumbs and chocolate chips.

6. Cover and cook on Low for 2½–3 hours or until edges are done and pudding is bubbly.

Chocolate Peanut Butter Cake

Janeen Troyer, Fairview, MI

Prep. Time: 15 minutes   Cooking Time: 1½ hours   Ideal slow-cooker size: 3-qt.

⅓ cup milk
¼ cup peanut butter
1 Tbsp. oil
½ tsp. vanilla extract
¾ cup white sugar, *divided*
½ cup flour
¾ tsp. baking powder
2 Tbsp. cocoa powder
1 cup boiling water

1. Spray the inside of the crock with nonstick spray.

2. Inside the crock, mix milk, peanut butter, oil, and vanilla together. Beat well.

3. Mix ¼ cup sugar, flour, and baking powder together into the batter in the crock and mix until just combined.

4. In bowl combine cocoa powder and the remaining ½ cup of sugar. Add water, stirring until well mixed, and dump slowly into the slow cooker. DO NOT STIR.

5. Cover and cook on High 1½ hours.

Serving Suggestion:
This is a favorite to eat with vanilla ice cream.

Chocolate Peanut Butter Dump Cake

Makes 8–10 servings

Esther Hartzler, Carlsbad, NM

Prep. Time: 7 minutes ❧ *Cooking Time: 2–2½ hours* ❧ *Ideal slow-cooker size: 5- to 6-qt.*

2 cups dry milk chocolate cake mix

½ cup water

6 Tbsp. peanut butter

2 eggs

½ cup chopped nuts

1. Combine all ingredients in electric mixer bowl. Beat for 2 minutes.

2. Spray interior of a baking insert designed to fit into your slow cooker with nonstick spray. Flour interior of greased insert. Pour batter into insert. Place insert in slow cooker.

3. Cover insert with 8 paper towels.

4. Cover cooker. Cook on High 2–2½ hours, or until toothpick inserted into center of cake comes out clean.

5. Allow cake to cool. Then invert onto a serving plate, cut, and serve.

Chocolate Peanut Butter Swirl Dump Cake

Makes 8–10 servings

Hope Comerford, Clinton Township, MI

Prep. Time: 10 minutes ⚬ *Cooking Time: 2–4 hours* ⚬ *Ideal slow-cooker size: 3½- to 4-qt.*

15¼-oz. box chocolate cake mix

3.4-oz. box butterscotch instant pudding

1¾ cups milk

4 1½-oz. pkgs. Reese's Peanut Butter Cups, chopped

¼ cup peanut butter

1. Spray crock with nonstick spray.

2. In a bowl, mix together the first three ingredients, then dump them into the crock.

3. Sprinkle chopped Reese's over the top of the batter, then swirl the peanut butter in with a spoon.

4. Cover and cook on Low for 2–4 hours.

Peanut Butter Cake

Makes 6 servings

Velma Sauder, Leola, PA

Prep. Time: 5–10 minutes ⚘ *Cooking Time: 2–3 hours* ⚘ *Ideal slow-cooker size: 4-qt.*

2 cups yellow cake mix

⅓ cup crunchy peanut butter

½ cup water

1. Combine all ingredients in bowl. Beat with electric mixer about 2 minutes.

2. Pour batter into greased and floured crock.

3. Cover insert with 8 paper towels, then cover with lid. Cook on High 2–3 hours, or until toothpick inserted into center of cake comes out clean. About 30 minutes before the end of the cooking time, remove the cooker's lid, but keep the paper towels in place.

4. When cake is fully cooked, remove insert from slow cooker. Turn insert upside down on a serving plate and remove cake.

No-Fuss Carrot Dump Cake

Makes 12–14 servings

Hope Comerford, Clinton Township, MI

Prep. Time: 15 minutes & Cooking Time: 3½–4 hours & Ideal slow-cooker size: 6-qt.

18¼-oz. box spice cake mix
2 cups shredded carrots
15½-oz. can crushed pineapple
3 eggs
⅓ cup oat flour
¼ cup raisins

1. Spray crock with nonstick spray.

2. Mix all ingredients together in a bowl and pour into the crock.

3. Cover and cook on Low for 3½–4 hours.

Sunny Spice Dump Cake

Makes 10–12 servings

Phyllis Good, Lancaster, PA

Prep. Time: 15 minutes ☙ Cooking Time: 2½–3½ hours ☙ Ideal slow-cooker size: 5-qt.

18¼-oz. box spice cake mix

3.4-oz. box butterscotch instant pudding

2 cups milk

2 eggs

10–12 fresh or canned peach halves, drained if canned

9-oz. container frozen whipped topping, thawed

1. Grease and flour interior of slow cooker crock.

2. In a mixing bowl, blend together cake mix, pudding mix, milk, and eggs.

3. Pour into prepared crock, spreading batter out evenly.

4. Cover. Bake on High 2½–3½ hours, or until tester inserted into center of cake comes out clean.

5. Uncover, being careful not to let condensation from inside of lid drip on finished cake.

6. Remove crock from cooker and let cool.

7. When ready to serve, cut into serving-size pieces. Place a peach half on each serving of cake. Top each with a dollop of whipped topping.

Pumpkin Dump Cake

Makes 8 servings

Janie Steele, Moore, OK

Prep. Time: 30 minutes ♣ *Cooking Time: 4–5 hours* ♣ *Ideal slow-cooker size: 6–qt.*

15-oz. can pumpkin puree
12 oz. evaporated milk
3 eggs
1 tsp. salt
1 cup sugar
3 tsp. cinnamon
15¼-oz. box yellow cake mix
1 cup chopped pecans
12 Tbsp. (1½ sticks) butter, melted

1. Mix pumpkin, milk, eggs, salt, sugar, and cinnamon together in a bowl.

2. Pour batter into greased slow cooker.

3. Sprinkle dry cake mix over top of mixture.

4. Sprinkle pecans over top.

5. Pour melted butter over top of mixture.

6. Cook 4–5 hours on Low.

Serving suggestion:
Serve with ice cream or whipped topping.

Pumpkin Pie Dump Cake

Makes 10–12 servings

Hope Comerford, Clinton Township, MI

Prep. Time: 15 minutes ⚶ Cooking Time: 3–5 hours ⚶ Ideal slow-cooker size: 3½- or 4-qt.

15-oz. can pumpkin puree
10-oz. can evaporated milk
½ cup brown sugar
3 tsp. pumpkin pie spice
⅛ tsp. nutmeg
18¾-oz. box yellow cake mix
1 cup graham cracker crumbs
½ cup white chocolate chips

1. Spray crock with nonstick spray.

2. In a bowl, mix together the first five ingredients and dump into the crock.

3. Sprinkle the cake mix over the batter in the crock, followed by the graham cracker crumbs and white chocolate chips.

4. Cover and cook on Low for 3–5 hours.

Pumpkin Pie Pudding

Makes 8 servings

Janie Steele, Moore, OK

Prep. Time: 30 minutes ⚘ *Cooking Time: 4–5 hours* ⚘ *Ideal slow-cooker size: 6-qt.*

15-oz. can pumpkin puree
12 oz. evaporated milk
3 eggs
1 tsp. salt
1 cup sugar
3 tsp. cinnamon
15¼-oz. box yellow cake mix
1 cup chopped pecans
12 Tbsp. (1½ sticks) butter, melted

1. Mix pumpkin, milk, eggs, salt, sugar, and cinnamon together in a bowl.

2. Pour batter into greased slow cooker.

3. Sprinkle dry cake mix over top of mixture.

4. Sprinkle pecans over top.

5. Pour melted butter over top of mixture.

6. Cook 4–5 hours on Low.

Serving suggestion:
Serve with ice cream or whipped topping.

Funfetti Dump Cake

Makes 8–10 servings

Hope Comerford, Clinton Township, MI

Prep. Time: 5 minutes ⚶ *Cooking Time: 3–5 hours* ⚶ *Ideal slow-cooker size: 3½- or 4-qt.*

15¼-oz. box Funfetti cake mix
3.4-oz. box vanilla instant pudding
2 cups milk
½ cup rainbow sprinkles

1. Spray crock with nonstick spray.

2. In a bowl, mix together the first three ingredients. Once blended, stir in the sprinkles, then dump in the crock.

3. Cover and cook on Low for 3–5 hours.

Spicy Chocolate Pumpkin Dump Cake

Makes 10–12 servings

Phyllis Good, Lancaster, PA

Prep. Time: 15–20 minutes ⚭ *Cooking Time: 3½–4 hours* ⚭ *Ideal slow-cooker size: 5-qt.*

18¼-oz. box spice cake mix

½ cup water

½ cup vegetable oil

3 large eggs

4 oz. cream cheese, softened

1 cup canned or cooked pumpkin

6 squares semisweet baking chocolate, coarsely chopped

1. Grease and flour interior of slow cooker crock.

2. Using an electric mixer, blend together cake mix, water, oil, and eggs.

3. Blend in cream cheese and pumpkin, beating on medium speed.

4. Stir in chopped chocolate.

5. Pour into prepared crock, smoothing it out evenly.

6. Cover. Bake on High 3½–4 hours, or until tester inserted into center of cake comes out clean.

7. Uncover, making sure condensation on inside of lid doesn't drip on finished cake.

8. Remove crock from cooker and allow cake to cool.

Fruity Dump Desserts

White Chocolate Berry Dump Cake

Makes 6 servings

Hope Comerford, Clinton Township, MI

Prep. Time: 15 minutes ⚬ *Cooking Time: 6 hours* ⚬ *Ideal slow-cooker size: 3-qt.*

2 cups frozen mixed berries

2 tsp. vanilla extract

¼–½ cup brown sugar

18¼-oz. box yellow butter cake mix
(or use plain white or yellow)

8 Tbsp. (1 stick) butter, melted

¼–½ cup white chocolate chips

3 Tbsp. water

1. Spray the inside of your crock with nonstick cooking spray.

2. Pour the mixed berries in the bottom of the slow cooker and top with the vanilla and brown sugar.

3. In a medium-sized bowl, mix the cake mix and butter, then stir in the white chocolate chips. Pour this over the mixed berries in the crock.

4. Cover and cook on Low for 6 hours.

Blackberry Dump Cake

Makes 8-10 servings

Hope Comerford, Clinton Township, MI

Prep. Time: 15 minutes   Cooking Time: 3–5 hours   Ideal slow-cooker size: 3½- or 4-qt.

15-oz. box yellow cake mix
3 oz. box blackberry gelatin mix
8 Tbsp. (1 stick) butter, melted
1 cup water
4 cups blackberries

1. Spray crock with nonstick spray.

2. In a bowl, mix the first four ingredients together. Once blended, gently fold in the blackberries, then dump the batter into the crock.

3. Cover and cook on Low for 3–5 hours.

Gluten-Free Raspberry Dump Cake

Makes 12 servings

Hope Comerford, Clinton Township, MI

Prep. Time: 5 minutes   Cooking Time: 4 hours   Ideal slow-cooker size: 5-qt.

2 21-oz. cans raspberry pie filling

1 15–17-oz. box gluten-free yellow cake mix

8 Tbsp. (1 stick) butter, melted

¼ cup confectioners' sugar, *optional*

1. Spray crock with nonstick spray.

2. Dump both cans of raspberry pie filling into crock and spread evenly.

3. Mix together the yellow cake mix with the butter, then spread evenly over the top of the raspberry pie filling.

4. Cover and cook on Low for 4 hours.

5. Just before serving, sprinkle with confectioners' sugar, if desired.

Blueberry Swirl Dump Cake

Makes 10–12 servings

Phyllis Good, Lancaster, PA

Prep. Time: 15–20 minutes ⚬ Cooking Time: 3½–4 hours ⚬ Ideal slow-cooker size: 5-qt.

3-oz. pkg. cream cheese, softened
18¼-oz. box white cake mix
3 eggs
3 Tbsp. water
21-oz. can blueberry pie filling

1. Grease and flour interior of slow cooker crock.

2. Beat cream cheese in a large mixing bowl until soft and creamy.

3. Stir in dry cake mix, eggs, and water. Blend well with cream cheese.

4. Pour batter into prepared crock, spreading it out evenly.

5. Pour blueberry pie filling over top of batter.

6. Swirl blueberries and batter by zigzagging a table knife through the batter.

7. Cover. Bake on High 3½–4 hours, or until a tester inserted into center of cake comes out clean.

8. Uncover, being careful to not let condensation from lid drop on finished cake.

9. Remove crock from cooker.

10. Serve cake warm or at room temperature.

Cherry Delight Dump Cake

Makes 10–12 servings

Anna Musser, Manheim, PA
Marianne J. Troyer, Millersburg, OH

Prep. Time: 5 minutes ⚶ *Cooking Time: 2–4 hours* ⚶ *Ideal slow-cooker size: 5-qt.*

21-oz. can cherry pie filling
1 box yellow cake mix
8 Tbsp. (1 stick) butter, melted
⅓ cup walnuts, *optional*

1. Place pie filling in greased slow cooker.

2. Combine dry cake mix and butter (mixture will be crumbly). Sprinkle over filling. Sprinkle with walnuts.

3. Cover and cook on Low 4 hours, or on High 2 hours.

 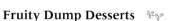

Cherry Dump Dessert

Makes 8 servings

Anita Troyer, Fairview, MI
Charlotte Shaffer, East Earl, PA

Prep. Time: 10 minutes ⚬ *Cooking Time: 2 hours* ⚬ *Ideal slow-cooker size: 4-qt.*

2 21-oz. cans cherry pie filling
18-oz. box white cake mix
12 Tbsp. (1½ sticks) butter, melted

1. Place the cherry filling into crock.

2. Pour cake mix onto cherries.

3. Drizzle melted butter over top, taking care to cover as much surface as possible.

4. Cover and cook on High for 2 hours.

Serving suggestion:

May serve as is or with milk or ice cream.

Variation:

You may use chocolate cake mix instead of white for a chocolate cherry dessert.

Cherry Dump Cake

Makes 8 servings

Jennifer Freed, Rockingham, VA

Prep. Time: 5 minutes ⚬ *Cooking Time: 2–4 hours* ⚬ *Ideal slow-cooker size: 5- or 6-qt.*

2 21-oz. cans cherry pie filling

1 tsp. almond extract, *divided*

18-oz. box yellow cake mix

8 Tbsp. (1 stick) salted butter, melted

1. Spray crock with nonstick cooking spray.

2. Stir ½ tsp. almond extract into each can of pie filling.

3. Pour both cans of cherry pie filling into prepared crock.

4. Sprinkle yellow cake mix evenly over cherry pie filling.

5. Slowly pour melted butter all over the top of the cake mix.

6. Cook on Low for 4 hours or High for 2 hours.

Cherry Pineapple Dump Cake

Makes 6 servings

Shelia Heil, Lancaster, PA

Prep. Time: 10 minutes ⚬ Cooking Time: 3 hours ⚬ Ideal slow-cooker size: 4-qt.

21-oz. can cherry pie filling
8-oz. can pineapple tidbits, drained
18¼-oz. box yellow cake mix
½ cup oil

1. Grease crock.

2. In a small bowl, mix the cherry pie filling and pineapple tidbits. Dump mixture in crock.

3. Evenly spread the box of dry cake mix over the pie filling mixture.

4. Pour oil evenly over the top of the dry cake mix.

5. Place a paper towel over the top of the crock and secure it with the lid.

6. Cook on Low for about 3 hours.

Serving suggestion:

Delicious served warm. May add ice cream or whipped cream if you choose.

Variation:

If you prefer a peach cobbler dump cake, use 2 16-oz. cans peaches in heavy syrup, an 18¼-oz. box yellow cake mix, ½ cup oil, and ½ tsp. ground cinnamon. Cut peaches into chunks and then prepare using same method as above.

Cherry Walnut Delight

Makes 6 servings

Janie Steele, Moore, OK

Prep. Time: 20 minutes   ❧   *Cooking Time: 4 hours*   ❧   *Ideal slow-cooker size: 6-qt.*

20-oz. can cherry pie filling (can use sugar free)

8 Tbsp. (1 stick) butter, melted

18-oz. box yellow cake mix

⅓ cup chopped walnuts

1. Place pie filling in greased slow cooker.

2. Mix melted butter in dry cake mix.

3. Sprinkle over top of pie filling.

4. Sprinkle chopped walnuts over the top of the cake.

5. Cover cook on Low 4 hours.

Serving Suggestion:

Serve with ice cream or whipped topping.

Cherry Cheesecake

Makes 8 servings

Susan Kasting, Jenks, OK

Prep. Time: 7 minutes ⚬ Cooking Time: 2 hours ⚬ Ideal slow-cooker size: 5-qt.

8 oz. cream cheese
¼ cup sugar
2 21-oz. cans cherry pie filling
15¼ oz. yellow cake mix
8 Tbsp. (1 stick) butter, melted

1. Mix cream cheese and sugar.

2. Pour cherry pie filling into greased slow cooker.

3. Top filling with cream cheese mixture, as evenly as possible.

4. Sprinkle cake mix over fillings in crock.

5. Pour butter over cake mix.

6. Cook on Low for 2 hours.

Cherry Cobbler Spoon Dessert

Makes 8 servings

Marla Folkerts, Batavia, IL

Prep. Time: 5 minutes   ♣   Cooking Time: 2 hours   ♣   Ideal slow-cooker size: 4-qt.

18¼-oz. box cherry chip-flavored cake mix

20-oz. can cherry pie filling

1. Spray the slow cooker crock with cooking spray.

2. Spread half of the cake mix in the bottom of the slow cooker.

3. Spread half the can of pie filling over the dry cake mix.

4. Repeat the layers.

5. Cover and cook on High for 2 hours.

6. Do not invert. Serve directly from the slow cooker with a spoon.

Cherry Pie Crisp

Makes 8 servings

Carrie Fritz, Meridian, ID

Prep. Time: 15 minutes ⚬ *Cooking Time: 3–4 hours* ⚬ *Ideal slow-cooker size: 3- or 4-qt.*

21-oz. can of cherry pie filling
⅔ cup brown sugar
½ cup flour
½ cup old-fashioned oats
1 tsp. vanilla extract
5⅓ Tbsp. (⅓ cup) butter

1. Dump cherry pie filling in a greased slow cooker.

2. In a separate bowl mix together brown sugar, flour, oats, and vanilla. Cut in butter until crumbles form.

3. Sprinkle oat mixture over the cherry pie filling.

4. Cover and cook on Low 3–4 hours. A paper towel can be placed under the lid to help absorb moisture.

Serving suggestion:

Serve warm with vanilla ice cream.

Caramel Apple Pie Dump Cake

Makes 8 servings

Hope Comerford, Clinton Township, MI

Prep. Time: 8 minutes   ♣   Cooking Time: 5–6 hours   ♣   Ideal slow-cooker size: 5-qt.

21-oz. can caramel apple pie filling

½ cup old-fashioned oats

15-oz. box gluten-free yellow cake mix (you can also use non-gluten-free cake mix)

⅓ cup brown sugar

1 tsp. cinnamon

5 Tbsp. butter, melted

1. Line crock with parchment paper.

2. Spread apple caramel pie filling around the bottom of the crock.

3. Sprinkle the oats all over the pie filling, followed by the cake mix, then brown sugar, then cinnamon.

4. Pour the melted butter evenly over contents of the crock.

5. Cover and cook on Low for 5–6 hours.

Caramel Apple Dump Cake

Makes 6–8 servings

Janie Steele, Moore, OK
Charlotte Shaffer, East Earl, PA

Prep. Time: 10 minutes ❧ *Cooking Time: 4 hours* ❧ *Ideal slow-cooker size: 6-qt.*

2 21-oz. cans apple pie filling (can use sugar-free)
½ cup caramel ice cream topping
15¼-oz. box yellow cake mix
8 Tbsp. (1 stick) butter, melted

1. Pour pie filling into slow cooker.

2. Drizzle caramel topping over pie filling.

3. Combine cake mix and butter in a bowl.

4. Sprinkle cake mixture over top of apple mixture.

5. Cover and cook on Low for 4 hours.

Serving suggestion:
  Serve with ice cream or whipped topping.

Spiced Apple Dump Cake

Makes 6–8 servings

Janie Steele, Moore, OK

Prep. Time: 20 minutes ❧ Cooking Time: 4 hours ❧ Ideal slow-cooker size: 6-qt.

2 21-oz. cans apple pie filling (can use sugar-free)

2 tsp. cinnamon

15¼-oz. box spice cake mix

8 Tbsp. (1 stick) butter, melted

1. Pour pie filling into greased slow cooker.

2. Sprinkle cinnamon over top.

3. Mix cake mix and butter in a bowl.

4. Pour mixture over apples.

5. Cook on Low 4 hours.

Serving suggestion:
Serve with ice cream or whipped topping.

Apple Harvest Delight

Marla Folkerts, Batavia, IL

Prep. Time: 10 minutes ⚬ *Cooking Time: 2 hours* ⚬ *Ideal slow-cooker size: 4-qt.*

18¼-oz. box French vanilla cake mix

1 tsp. ground cinnamon

½ tsp. ground cloves

1 cup quick-cooking oats

21-oz. can cinnamon spice apple pie filling

1. Preheat the slow cooker on High for 10 minutes.

2. Spray the slow cooker with cooking spray.

3. In a large bowl, stir together the dry cake mix, cinnamon, cloves, and dry oats until well mixed.

4. Insert a sharp knife into an open can of apple pie filling and cut the apples into small pieces.

5. Spread one cup of the dry cake mix on bottom of the slow cooker.

6. Spread half the can of apple pie filling over the dry cake mix.

7. Spread 2 cups of the dry cake mixture over the pie filling.

8. Spread the remaining pie filling over the second layer of dry cake mixture.

9. Spread the remaining dry cake mixture over the pie filling.

10. Spray the top with cooking spray.

11. Cover and cook on High for 2 hours.

12. Serve directly from the slow cooker. Do not invert.

Cranberry Apple Dump Cake

Makes 6 servings

Charlotte Shaffer, East Earl, PA

Prep. Time: 5 minutes   ⚜   *Cooking Time: 2–4 hours*   ⚜   *Ideal slow-cooker size: 5-qt.*

21-oz. can apple pie filling

14-oz. can whole berry cranberry sauce

15¼-oz. box yellow cake mix

8 Tbsp. (1 stick) butter, melted

1. In a greased crock, stir together the apple pie filling and cranberry sauce.

2. Spread the mixture evenly around.

3. In medium bowl, combine cake mix and melted butter and stir until crumbly.

4. Pour the cake/butter mixture over cranberry/apple mixture in crock.

5. Cover with lid.

6. Cook on High for 2 hours or on Low for 4 hours.

Cran Apple Crunch

Makes 8 servings

Susan Kasting, Jenks, OK

Prep. Time: 10 minutes ♣ *Cooking Time: 2 hours* ♣ *Ideal slow-cooker size: 5-qt.*

2 21-oz. cans apple pie filling
⅓ cup dried cranberries
15¼-oz. box spice cake mix
8 Tbsp. (1 stick) butter, melted
3 Tbsp. cinnamon sugar
½ cup walnut pieces

1. Grease slow cooker.

2. Mix apple pie filling and cranberries in slow cooker.

3. Mix cake mix and butter together in a bowl.

4. Sprinkle cake mix evenly over pie filling.

5. Sprinkle nuts and cinnamon sugar over cake mix.

6. Cover and cook for 2 hours on Low.

Apple Crisp

Makes 4 servings

Carrie Fritz, Meridian, ID

Prep. Time: 15 minutes & Cooking Time: 3–4 hours & Ideal slow-cooker size: 4- or 5-qt.

2 lbs. apples
⅔ cup old-fashioned oats
⅔ cup flour
⅔ cup brown sugar
½ tsp. cinnamon
¼ tsp. nutmeg
pinch salt
6 Tbsp. butter

1. Peel and slice the apples. Place in a greased slow cooker.

2. Combine the rest of the ingredients except for butter in a separate bowl.

3. Cut butter into the rest of the dry ingredients.

4. Sprinkle the topping over the apples.

5. Cook on Low for 3–4 hours.

Serving suggestion:
Serve warm with vanilla ice cream or whipped cream.

Gingerbread Apple Cobbler

Makes 6–8 servings

Janie Steele, Moore, OK

Prep. Time: 15 minutes ⚬ Cooking Time: 4–5 hours ⚬ Ideal slow-cooker size: 6-qt.

2 21-oz. cans apple pie filling (can use sugar-free)

4 Tbsp. (½ stick) butter, melted

14½-oz. box gingerbread mix (batter prepared according to directions on box)

1. Grease the inside of the crock.

2. Pour the apple pie filling and melted butter into the crock and stir.

3. Pour the prepared gingerbread mix over the top of the apples.

4. Cover and cook on Low for 4–5 hours.

Serving suggestion:

Serve with ice cream or whipped topping.

Apple German Chocolate Dump Cake

Makes 10–12 servings

Phyllis Good, Lancaster, PA

Prep. Time: 15–20 minutes ⚬ *Cooking Time: 3½–4 hours* ⚬ *Ideal slow-cooker size: 5-qt.*

21-oz. can apple pie filling

18¼-oz. box German chocolate cake mix

3 eggs

¾ cup coarsely chopped walnuts

½ cup miniature semisweet chocolate chips

1. Grease and flour interior of slow cooker crock.

2. Place pie filling in blender or food processor. Cover and process until apples are in ¼-inch chunks.

3. If using food processor, add dry cake mix and eggs. Process until smooth. (If you used a blender for the apples, pour them into an electric mixer bowl, add dry cake mix and eggs, and beat on medium speed for 5 minutes.)

4. Pour into prepared slow cooker crock.

5. Sprinkle with walnuts and chocolate chips.

6. Cover. Bake on High 3½–4 hours, or until tester inserted into center of cake comes out clean.

7. Remove crock from cooker. Allow to cool completely before serving.

Simply Apple Dump Cake

Make 10–12 servings

Hope Comerford, Clinton Township, MI

Prep. Time: 10 minutes ❧ Cooking Time: 3–5 hours ❧ Ideal slow-cooker size: 3½- or 4-qt.

21-oz. can apple pie filling
18¾-oz. box yellow cake mix
8 Tbsp. (1 stick) butter, melted

1. Spray crock with nonstick spray.

2. Dump apple pie filling into crock.

3. In a bowl, mix together the yellow cake mix and melted butter. Spoon this into the crock.

4. Cover and cook on Low for 3–5 hours.

Sour Cream Peach Dump Cake

Makes 10–12 servings

Phyllis Good, Lancaster, PA

Prep. Time: 15 minutes   ❧   Cooking Time: 3½–4 hours   ❧   Ideal slow-cooker size: 5-qt.

18¼-oz. box orange-flavored cake mix

21-oz. can peach pie filling

½ cup sour cream

2 eggs

confectioners' sugar or whipped topping

1. Grease and flour interior of slow cooker crock.

2. Mix dry cake mix, pie filling, sour cream, and eggs together until thoroughly blended.

3. Pour batter into prepared crock, spreading it out evenly.

4. Cover. Bake on High 3½–4 hours, or until tester inserted into center of cake comes out clean.

5. Remove crock from cooker and allow to cool to room temperature.

6. Sprinkle cake with confectioners' sugar, or spread with whipped topping just before serving.

Spiced Peach Dump Cake

Makes 10–12 servings

Hope Comerford, Clinton Township, MI

Prep. Time: 15 minutes ❧ *Cooking Time: 3–5 hours* ❧ *Ideal slow-cooker size: 3½- or 4-qt.*

21-oz. can peach pie filling
18¾-oz. box spice cake mix
8 Tbsp. (1 stick) butter, melted

1. Spray crock with nonstick spray.

2. Dump peach pie filling into crock.

3. In a bowl, mix together the spice cake mix and melted butter. Spoon this into the crock.

4. Cover and cook on Low for 3–5 hours.

Old-Fashioned Peach Crisp

Makes 4 servings

Carrie Fritz, Meridian, ID

Prep. Time: 15 minutes ⚬ *Cooking Time: 3 hours* ⚬ *Ideal slow-cooker size: 4- to 5-qt.*

2 lbs. peeled and sliced peaches
⅔ cup old-fashioned oats
⅔ cup flour
⅔ cup brown sugar
½ tsp. cinnamon
¼ tsp. nutmeg
pinch salt
6 Tbsp. butter

1. Place peeled and sliced peaches in a greased slow cooker.

2. In a separate bowl mix together the rest of the ingredients except butter.

3. Cut butter into the dry ingredients.

4. Sprinkle oat mixture over the top of the peaches.

5. Cook on Low for 3 hours.

Serving suggestion:
Good served warm with vanilla ice cream.

Favorite memory of sharing this recipe:
We make this every summer with peaches fresh from the orchard.

Peach Crisp

Makes 4–6 servings

Janie Steele, Moore, OK

Prep. Time: 20 minutes ⚬ Cooking Time: 4–5 hours ⚬ Ideal slow-cooker size: 5-qt.

¼ cup biscuit mix
⅔ cup quick or rolled oats
1½ tsp. cinnamon
¾ cup brown sugar
4 cups canned peaches, cut in chunks
½ cup peach juice

1. Mix biscuit mix, oats, cinnamon, and brown sugar in a bowl.

2. Place peaches and juice in bottom of greased slow cooker.

3. Add dry ingredients over top of peaches.

4. Stir slightly to gently coat peaches.

5. Cook on Low 3½–4½ hours covered, then remove lid for the last 30 minutes.

Serving suggestion:

Serve with ice cream or whipped topping.

Peach Crumble

Makes 4 servings

Anita Troyer, Fairview, MI

Prep. Time: 20 minutes ⚭ Cooking Time: 2 hours ⚭ Ideal slow-cooker size: 4-qt.

Crumbs
1¼ cups flour
¾ cup white sugar
1½ tsp. baking powder
¼ tsp. salt
2 Tbsp. butter
8 peaches or 4 cups peaches, peeled, sliced
4 Tbsp. butter, melted

1. Mix crumb ingredients together and work into a crumb mixture. Set aside.

2. Into bottom of greased crock, put peaches.

3. Put ½ cup of crumb mixture into the peaches and mix well.

4. Sprinkle the rest of the crumbs on top of the peaches.

5. Drizzle the 4 Tbsp. melted butter over the peaches.

6. Cover and cook on High for 2 hours.

Serving suggestion:
Serve with milk or ice cream.

Lightly White Pear Dump Cake

Makes 10–12 servings

Phyllis Good, Lancaster, PA

Prep. Time: 15–20 minutes ⚬ *Cooking Time: 3 ½–4 hours* ⚬ *Ideal slow-cooker size: 5-qt.*

15¼-oz. can pears (you're going to chop them, so buy pear pieces if you can find them)

18¼-oz. pkg. white cake mix

1 egg

2 egg whites

2 tsp. confectioners' sugar

1. Grease and flour interior of slow cooker crock.

2. Fish pears out of syrup to chop them, but keep the syrup.

3. Place chopped pears and syrup into electric mixing bowl. Add dry cake mix, egg, and egg whites.

4. Beat with electric mixer on low speed for 30 seconds, and then on high speed for 4 minutes.

5. Spoon batter into prepared crock, spreading it out evenly.

6. Cover cooker. Bake on High 3½–4 hours, or until tester inserted in center of cake comes out clean.

7. Uncover without letting condensation drip on cake. Remove crock from cooker. Allow to cool completely.

8. Dust with confectioners' sugar before slicing or spooning out to serve.

Lemon Dump Cake

Makes 6 servings

Janie Steele, Moore, OK

Prep. Time: 10 minutes ⚭ *Cooking Time: 4 hours* ⚭ *Ideal slow-cooker size: 6-qt.*

2 15¾-oz. cans lemon pie filling

15¼-oz. box lemon cake mix

8 Tbsp. (1 stick) butter, melted

1. Pour pie filling in greased slow cooker.

2. Mix cake mix and melted butter together in a bowl.

3. Sprinkle cake mixture over pie filling.

4. Cook 4 hours on Low.

Serving suggestion:
Serve with whipped topping.

Lemon Raspberry Dump Cake

Makes 8 servings

Hope Comerford, Clinton Township, MI

Prep. Time: 10 minutes ⚬ *Cooking Time: 3½–4½ hours* ⚬ *Ideal slow-cooker size: 3-qt.*

3.9-oz. box lemon pudding mix

15¼-oz. box yellow cake mix, batter prepared according to box directions

1 cup black or red raspberries

powdered sugar for dusting at serving

1. Spray crock with nonstick spray.

2. Stir the lemon pudding mix into the yellow cake batter.

3. Gently fold the raspberries into the cake mix/ pudding mixture.

4. Pour this mixture into your crock. Cover and cook on Low for 3½–4½ hours with paper towel under the lid to catch the condensation.

5. Let the cake cool completely. Run a knife around the edge, then turn your crock upside down on a plate or platter. Dust the cake lightly with powdered sugar before serving if desired.

Lemon Pear Gingerbread Delight

Makes 6 servings

Sue Hamilton, Benson, AZ

Prep. Time: 5 minutes   ☆   Cooking Time: 3 hours   ☆   Ideal slow-cooker size: 7-qt.

21-oz. can of lemon cream pie filling

29-oz. can of sliced pears, drained

14½-oz. package of gingerbread cake and cookie mix

16 Tbsp. (2 sticks) butter, cold

1. Spray the cooker with nonstick spray.

2. Spread the lemon filling in the bottom of the crock.

3. Put a layer of sliced pears over the filling.

4. Sprinkle the cookie mix on top of the fruit.

5. Cut the butter in slices and put on top of the mix.

6. Cover and cook on High for 3 hours.

Serving suggestion:

Let cool for 30 minutes before serving. Serve warm—or even better, ice cold.

Coconut Lime Dump Cake

Makes 8 servings

Hope Comerford, Clinton Township, MI

Prep. Time: 5 minutes & Cooking Time: 5–6 hours & Ideal slow-cooker size: 5-qt.

22-oz. can key lime crème pie filling and topping

2 tsp. lime zest

½ cup shredded coconut

15-oz. gluten-free yellow cake mix (may use non-gluten-free cake mix)

4 Tbsp. coconut oil, melted

1. Line crock with parchment paper.

2. Spread key lime crème pie filling and topping over bottom of crock.

3. Sprinkle lime zest and shredded coconut over pie filling.

4. Sprinkle cake mix over the top of the contents of the crock.

5. Pour the melted coconut oil evenly over the top of the cake mix.

6. Cover and cook on Low 5–6 hours.

Key Lime Dump Cake

Makes 8 servings

Janie Steele, Moore, OK
Jennifer Freed, Rockingham, VA

Prep. Time: 5 minutes ❧ Cooking Time: 2 hours ❧ Ideal slow-cooker size: 5- or 6-qt.

2 22-oz. cans key lime pie filling
15¼-oz. box French vanilla cake mix
8 Tbsp. (1 stick) butter, melted

1. Spray inside of crock with nonstick cooking spray.

2. Empty cans of key lime pie filling into bottom of crock, then spread out evenly.

3. In medium mixing bowl, combine dry vanilla cake mix and butter, then stir until crumbly (break up any large chunks into small crumbles with spoon).

4. Pour cake/butter crumble mixture over pie filling, spread out evenly, and cover crock with lid.

5. Cook on High for 2 hours, or Low for 4 hours.

Serving suggestion:
Serve with whipped cream or ice cream.

Rhubarb Dump Cake

Makes 6–8 servings

Genelle Taylor, Perrysburg, OH

Prep. Time: 10 minutes ⚜ *Cooking Time: about 3 hours* ⚜ *Ideal slow-cooker size: 5- or 6-qt.*

4 cups chopped rhubarb
1 cup sugar
3-oz. box strawberry gelatin mix
15¼-oz. box white cake mix
1 cup water
5⅓ Tbsp. (⅓ cup) butter, melted

1. Grease slow cooker with butter or nonstick spray.

2. Place rhubarb in slow cooker. Sprinkle with sugar, gelatin, and cake mix.

3. Add water.

4. Drizzle butter over the top.

5. Cover and cook on High about 3 hours.

Favorite memory of sharing this recipe:
   Those of us who don't normally care for rhubarb LOVE this cake!

Variation:
   It can also be baked for 1 hour in a 350°F oven.

Rhubarb Crunch

Makes 4–6 servings

Janeen Troyer, Fairview, MI

Prep. Time: 20 minutes ❧ Cooking Time: 2 hours ❧ Ideal slow-cooker size: 3-qt.

I cup flour

¼ cup quick oats

¾ cup brown sugar

5 Tbsp. butter

I tsp. cinnamon

¾ cup white sugar

2 Tbsp. cornstarch

I tsp. vanilla extract

2 cups diced rhubarb

1. Crumble together flour, quick oats, brown sugar, butter, and cinnamon.

2. Pat half of the crumbs into the bottom of the slow cooker and set the other half aside.

3. Combine white sugar, cornstarch, and vanilla in a 2-quart microwave bowl and stir until smooth.

4. Add rhubarb to the water mixture and cover. Microwave on High for 2 minutes. Stir. Microwave again for 2 minutes at a time until mixture becomes thick and clear.

5. Pour rhubarb mixture over the crumbs in the crock and then crumble the remaining crumbs over the top.

6. Cover and bake on High for 1 hour.

7. Uncover and bake for an additional 30 minutes to an hour or until the top is crunchy. Allow it to cool before eating.

Serving suggestion:
Goes well with vanilla ice cream.

Variation:
Can also be made with strawberries or ground cherries.

Mango Cornbread Cake

Makes 6 servings

Sue Hamilton, Benson, AZ

Prep. Time: 5 minutes & *Cooking Time: 2 hours* & *Ideal slow-cooker size: 7-qt.*

14 oz. mango puree (if frozen, thaw)

⅓ cup honey

2 15-oz. cans mango slices, drained

1 lb. Southwest cornbread mix (spicy pepper mix)

16 Tbsp. (2 sticks) butter, cold

1. Spread the mango puree in bottom of the crock.

2. Pour the honey over the puree.

3. Add the sliced mango on top.

4. Sprinkle the cornbread mix evenly over it.

5. Cut the butter into thin slices and place over the mix.

6. Cover and cook on High for 2 hours.

Serving suggestion:

Can be served warm, but even better ice cold.

Metric Equivalent Measurements

dash = little less than $\frac{1}{8}$ tsp.

3 tsp. = 1 Tbsp.

2 Tbsp. = 1 oz.

4 Tbsp. = ¼ cup

5 Tbsp. plus 1 tsp. = $\frac{1}{3}$ cup

8 Tbsp. = ½ cup

12 Tbsp. = ¾ cup

16 Tbsp. = 1 cup

1 cup = 8 oz. liquid

2 cups = 1 pt.

4 cups = 1 qt.

4 qt. = 1 gal.

1 stick butter = ¼ lb.

1 stick butter = ½ cup

1 stick butter = 8 Tbsp.

beans, 1 lb. dried = 2–2½ cups (depending on the size of the beans)

bell pepper, 1 large = 1 cup chopped

cheese, hard (for example, cheddar, Swiss, Monterey Jack, mozzarella), 1 lb. grated = 4 cups

cheese, cottage, 1 lb. = 2 cups

chocolate chips, 6-oz. pkg. = 1 scant cup

crackers (butter, saltines, snack), 20 single crackers = 1 cup crumbs

herbs, 1 Tbsp. fresh = 1 tsp. dried

lemon, 1 medium-sized = 2–3 Tbsp. juice

lemon, 1 medium-sized = 2–3 tsp. grated rind

mustard, 1 Tbsp. prepared = 1 tsp. dry or ground mustard

oatmeal, 1 lb. dry = about 5 cups dry

onion, 1 medium-sized = ½ cup chopped

Pasta

macaroni, penne, and other small or tubular shapes, 1 lb. dry = 4 cups uncooked

noodles, 1 lb. dry = 6 cups uncooked

spaghetti, linguine, fettucine, 1 lb. dry = 4 cups uncooked

potatoes, white, 1 lb. = 3 medium-sized potatoes = 2 cups mashed

Potatoes, sweet, 1 lb. = 3 medium-sized potatoes = 2 cups mashed

rice, 1 lb. dry = 2 cups uncooked

sugar, confectioners', 1 lb. = 3½ cups sifted

whipping cream, 1 cup unwhipped = 2 cups whipped

whipped topping, 8-oz. container = 3 cups

yeast, dry, 1 envelope (¼ oz.) = 1 Tbsp.

Assumptions about Ingredients

flour = unbleached or white, and all-purpose

oatmeal or oats = dry, quick or rolled (old-fashioned), unless specified

pepper = black, finely ground

rice = regular, long-grain (not instant unless specified)

salt = table salt

shortening = solid, not liquid

sugar = granulated sugar (not brown and not confectioners')

Substitute Ingredients

For 1 cup buttermilk—use 1 cup plain yogurt; or pour 1⅓ Tbsp. lemon juice or vinegar into a 1-cup measure. Fill the cup with milk. Stir and let stand for 5 minutes. Stir again before using.

For 1 oz. unsweetened baking chocolate—stir together 3 Tbsp. unsweetened cocoa powder and 1 Tbsp. butter, softened.

For 1 Tbsp. cornstarch—use 2 Tbsp. all-purpose flour; or 4 tsp. instant tapioca.

For 1 garlic clove—use ¼ tsp. garlic salt (reduce salt in recipe by ⅛ tsp.); or ⅛ tsp. garlic powder.

For 1 Tbsp. fresh herbs—use 1 tsp. dried herbs.

For 8 oz. fresh mushrooms—use 1 4-oz. can mushrooms, drained.

For 1 Tbsp. prepared mustard—use 1 tsp. dry or ground mustard.

For 1 medium-sized fresh onion—use 2 Tbsp. minced dried onion; or 2 tsp. onion salt (reduce salt in recipe by 1 tsp.); or 1 tsp. onion powder. Note: These substitutions will work for meatballs and meatloaf, but not for sautéing.

For 1 cup sour milk—use 1 cup plain yogurt; or pour 1 Tbsp. lemon juice or vinegar into a 1-cup measure. Fill with milk. Stir and then let stand for 5 minutes. Stir again before using.

For 2 Tbsp. tapioca—use 3 Tbsp. all-purpose flour.

For 1 cup canned tomatoes—use 1⅓ cups diced fresh tomatoes, cooked gently for 10 minutes.

For 1 Tbsp. tomato paste—use 1 Tbsp. ketchup.

For 1 Tbsp. vinegar—use 1 Tbsp. lemon juice.

For 1 cup heavy cream—add ¾ cup melted butter to ¾ cup milk. Note: This will work for baking and cooking, but not for whipping.

For 1 cup whipping cream—chill thoroughly ⅔ cup evaporated milk, plus the bowl and beaters, then whip; or use 2 cups store-bought whipped topping.

For ½ cup wine—pour 2 Tbsp. wine vinegar into a ½-cup measure. Fill with broth (chicken, beef, or vegetable). Stir and then let stand for 5 minutes. Stir again before using.

Recipe and Ingredient Index

About the Author

Hope Comerford is a mom, wife, elementary music teacher, blogger, recipe developer, public speaker, ALM Zone Fitness Motivator, Young Living Essential Oils essential oil enthusiast/educator, and published author. In 2013, she was diagnosed with a severe gluten intolerance and since then has spent many hours creating easy, practical, and delicious gluten-free recipes that can be enjoyed by both those who are affected by gluten and those who are not.

Growing up, Hope spent many hours in the kitchen with her Meme (grandmother) and her love for cooking grew from there. While working on her master's degree when her daughter was young, Hope turned to her slow cookers for some salvation and sanity. It was from there she began truly experimenting with recipes and quickly learned she had the ability to get a little more creative in the kitchen and develop her own recipes.

In 2010, Hope started her blog, *A Busy Mom's Slow Cooker Adventures*, to simply share the recipes she was making with her family and friends. She never imagined people all over the world would begin visiting her page and sharing her recipes with others as well. In 2013, Hope self-published her first cookbook, *Slow Cooker Recipes 10 Ingredients or Less and Gluten-Free* and then later wrote *The Gluten-Free Slow Cooker*.

Hope is thrilled to working with Fix-It and Forget-It and representing such an iconic line of cookbooks. She is excited to bring her creativeness to the Fix-It and Forget-It brand. Through Fix-It and Forget-It, Hope has written *Fix-It and Forget-It Lazy & Slow, Fix-It and Forget-It Healthy Slow Cooker Cookbook, Fix-It and Forget-It Favorite Slow Cooker Recipes for Mom, Fix-It and Forget-It Favorite Slow Cooker Recipes for Dad, Fix-It and Enjoy-It Welcome Home Cookbook, Fix-It and Forget-It Holiday Favorites, Fix-It, Forget-It Cooking for Two*, and *Fix-It and Forget-It Crowd Pleasers for the American Summer*.

Hope lives in the city of Clinton Township, Michigan, near Metro Detroit and is a Michigan native. She has been happily married to her husband and best friend, Justin, since 2008. Together they have two children, Ella and Gavin, who are her motivation, inspiration, and heart. In her spare time, Hope enjoys traveling, singing, cooking, reading books, spending time with friends and family, and relaxing.

FIX-IT and FORGET-IT®